Headwraps

Headwraps
A Global Journey

Georgia Scott

PublicAffairs

NEW YORK

Book Design by Jennifer Dossin. Text set in Photina.

Library of Congress Cataloging-in-Publication Data
Scott, Georgia.
Headwraps: a global journey / Georgia Scott.
p. cm.
Includes bibliographical references.
ISBN 1–58648–109–6
1. Headgear. 2. Veils. 3. Turbans. I. Title.
GT2110.S36 2003
931.4'3—dc22
2003060655
First Edition

10 9 8 7 6 5 4 3 2 1

To everyone with a dream and the drive to see it through.

Contents

Introduction

Was it Coco Chanel or my mother who said a woman should always
look her best? In my quest to do just that, I routinely stumbled with my hair. There were days, I'll admit, that I just couldn't get it together. But then help arrived in the form of a 1990s New York City fashion fad: women—especially black women—began wearing headwraps. They sprang up everywhere imaginable, from nightclubs to corporate offices. I'm not talking about the simple scarves women throw on their heads before rushing out to the supermarket. In New York, women were stepping out in towering, exotic headwraps made from yards of fabric in all varieties of color, texture, and pattern. These were architectural creations for the head.

I decided I wanted in on the trend. My attempts to learn how to tie my own headwraps inspired me to gather details for a small "trends" article for the *New York Times*, where I work in the art department. I interviewed women in cafes, on subway platforms, and anywhere else, asking them why they wore headwraps and how they came up with their individual styles. Each woman—all were black Americans who lived in New York City—said she wore a headwrap, in part, to identify with her African ancestry, and that her headwrap was "invented" from whim; she had no specific style. "I just stand in front of a mirror with a piece of fabric, and this is what I get," one said. She could have been speaking for them all. Many of them also boasted that their headwraps looked just like the turbans worn by kings and queens of Africa, which prompted me to ask, "From what countries in Africa?" I never got an answer to that question. "I don't know. Just Africa," they would say.

I decided I wanted to wear headwraps like the kings and queens in Africa, too, and set out to discover which wraps I should emulate. For that, I turned to immigrants from West Africa. I spoke to hair braiders from Senegal and Burkina Faso, street vendors from the Côte d'Ivoire, and shop owners from Nigeria. They all laughed when I told my story. No king, queen, chief, or anyone else would wear headwraps like those worn by Americans. First of all, men from the coastal region of West Africa don't wear turbans (they do in the Sudan, Mali, Niger, and other countries in the interior), and women wear very definitive styles that are nothing like the ones seen in America. Also, a West African woman would never wear a headwrap with Western clothes. And then there are detailed nuances in the design of West African headwraps—the way they're folded, tucked, and knotted—that give them a special visual flair. I was humbled. Not just because I had been informed that my newly embraced hair accessory was ugly, but because I didn't grasp the nuances in style they were talking about. I had adopted a fad that I didn't really understand.

I decided to investigate the origins of traditional West African style. I searched for insight in bookstores and libraries, but found none. I called professors at universities and got even less. There seemed to be no tangible information on traditional West African dress, or on the overall trend of headwraps. I did, however, discover in the *New York Times's* library a few books on traditional costumes, including two books written by R. Turner Wilcox in the 1960s, which contained information on many world cultures. Ms. Wilcox didn't go into detail about individual dress, but her books were filled with dozens of line drawings of indigenous costumes. That's when I realized that headwraps and headscarves are worn all over the world. At that point I was thirsty for more information, but nothing more existed. No one had written about headwraps.

That was in 1994. In 2000, I put in for a leave-of-absence, mapped out an itinerary, cashed in my stock, and bought a stack of plane tickets five inches thick. I moved everything out of my apartment and into a storage unit. I packed enough supplies into a backpack to last six months, shipped abroad supplies for another six months, and set off for my first country. For one year, from July 2000 to June 2001, I traveled around the world with the singular, determined purpose of documenting the world's headwraps and headscarves. Along the way, I got a rash from bedbugs, ate a heaping bowl of fresh fish-lip soup, took almost 4,000 photographs, and logged more than 55,000 miles of travel in planes, trains, and cars.

I had fun. Each country was absolutely different from the one before, and I had to adjust quickly to new currencies, languages, geography, climate, food, customs, and attitudes. I took furious notes, documenting everything I learned about one country and its traditional headgear before it could be wiped from my memory at the next stop.

Headwraps and headscarves are tremendously varied. They can be made of silk, cotton, gauze, muslin, wool, abaca, and many other fabrics. They can be tied, wrapped, pinned, folded, or twisted. They have hundreds of little nuances, from color and texture, to size and shape, to why they're worn and when. In some cultures, they have been wrapped the same way for generations, while other cultures create new styles every season. And they are worn for a variety of reasons. In many countries, such as India, Jamaica, Kenya, Ethiopia, and the United Arab Emirates, they are worn mainly for religious reasons. The way a headscarf is worn in the United Arab Emirates, for example, not only indicates a woman's country of origin, but also hints at her interpretation of the Qur'an and its edicts on feminine modesty. In other regions, headwraps reinforce social differences, distinguishing the wealthy from the poor, men from women, and clans from other clans. Or they mark major events. In some ethnic communities in rural China, for example, a headwrap indicates a woman's coming-of-age; the embroidery work on the turban of a young Yao woman in the mountains of Thailand indicates that she is able to make clothes for the family and is therefore ready for marriage. In some countries headwraps are an integral part of daily life. In Morocco, Mali, and Niger, for example, harsh climate conditions make headwraps a daily necessity, while in other countries, such as Indonesia and Malaysia, traditional headwraps are reserved for special occasions, such as weddings and official state functions.

Headwraps are dying out in many regions. The centuries-old practice of wearing headscarves in Russia and the Czech Republic, as well as turbans in Turkey, is gone. In Guatemala, Vietnam, China, and Thailand, headwraps are generally worn only by minority ethnic groups who live on the fringes of modern society. At the insistence of foreign invaders, many ethnic groups in the Philippines replaced their traditional dress with western clothes. They now have little interest in reviving the old ways.

Differences even extend to headwraps when they are *not* being used. When they aren't covering the head, headwraps and headscarves may double as towels, blankets, or ropes in some cultures, while in others the out-of-use fabric is considered sacred and is stored neatly in a drawer or passed on to the less fortunate.

Of course, each country's relationship with headwraps and headscarves is more complex than the brief summaries here, which is why this book is more than a picture book with captions. This book is an examination of the cultures of diverse peoples. Fabric is the common denominator.

Headwraps and headscarves are worn in at least 44 countries around the world. I traveled to 32. Within each country, I visited an average of three cities or towns and interviewed and/or photographed nearly everyone in my path. Starting with Morocco and Tunisia in the Sahara Desert of North Africa, and ending back in the United States, my travels fulfilled the first phase of an incredible adventure. This book marks its culmination.

Africa

The Sahara Desert
(Morocco and Tunisia)

For the first two days of my drive into the Sahara Desert, I saw most of southern Morocco's rust-colored mountains while lying on my back in the back seat of a 4x4. My ankle-length skirts were pulled up to my thighs and my sockless, shoeless feet dangled out the window. I'd left my hair loose so my bangs could flutter in the wind and had transformed my T-shirts into halter tops so the buildup of sweat wouldn't drench the fabric. That was my way of dealing with the heat, which could melt a frozen bottle of water and turn it disgustingly hot within a single hour. My casual style of dress was inappropriate for the region, however, so I covered myself up whenever we stopped in a town.

This covering and uncovering routine made me wonder what it would be like to be covered up all the time, like the Berber women I'd come to photograph. They would never allow their long, robe-like caftans to rise above their ankles, and most Moroccan women—Berber and Arab alike—keep their hair hidden underneath scarves when they go outside regardless of how hot it gets.

Berbers, the indigenous people of North Africa, are greatly influenced by Sharia, or Islamic law, which arrived around 682 with Arab invaders. Today, in an effort to "conceal their beauty" and appear modest in public, and when around men outside of their close family, women shroud themselves with a scarf or a shawl in much the same manner as Muslim

Page 2: A mock wedding ceremony at the Festival of Matmata in Tunisia; Page 3: Postcards of Berber women in Ouarzazate (left) and Zagora (right), southern Morocco.

women have done since the seventh century. Most Arab-Moroccan women wear silk, rayon, or polyester *hijabs*, scarves that cover the head, neck, and throat. In rural areas, many also wear *chadors*, a Persian word for large cloaks, and sometimes veils, that completely shroud a woman's frame.

Isolated Berber tribes—most of which live in the Riff, Middle Atlas, and High Atlas Mountains or the Sahara Desert—also wear scarves, known in different regions as *drras, zifs, foulards, tassfifts,* and by other French, Berber, or Arabic terms. Berber women in Morocco, Algeria, and Tunisia wore headscarves long before Arab merchants introduced Islam. Back then, women's head coverings weren't intrinsically related to religion, but as more and more Berber communities embraced Islam, their head coverings assumed a greater role.

In one Berber community I visited, a woman's modesty is so strictly enforced that when a mother of two was seen in public without a headscarf (she apparently had taken it off to adjust the style and was unwittingly photographed and made part of a film documentary), she lost her status in the community and her husband divorced her and took custody of their children. Two years later, when I arrived, the husband's brother said she still hadn't remarried or been fully accepted back into her old circle of friends.

Depending on the community, scarves are layered with as many as four pieces of fabric—from plain black squares of cotton with tassels or metal discs sewn along the edges to bright pieces of yellow and orange polyester or other soft material, with decorative tears along the fringe. They can be wrapped around like close-fitting turbans or draped loosely over the hair, with two ends tied in a single knot. Along with a caftan, Berber women usually wear a shawl—referred to by many tribes as a *haik*—and layers of amber and silver jewelry.

The complete ensemble is worn at different times in different regions, although in general it is reserved for special occasions, such as weddings. Unfortunately, no such occasions were scheduled along the route I traveled, so I had to commission

one. In the town of Merzouga, near Morocco's southeastern border with Algeria, my guide, with the help of a local shop owner, named Ali, made arrangements for an impromptu celebration. It was a mess. Ali turned out to be a pimp, and the four women he recruited were his prostitutes. Of course, none of this came to light until the last minute, when it was too late to start over. Thrilled to at least get a taste of traditional Berber dress and dance, I allowed the party to proceed.

Around 11 P.M., with miles of sand dunes towering in the distance, the performers claimed a dance area on a patch of sand in front of an *auberge*, or small hotel. The desert was pitch black, with the exception of a full moon, a blanket of stars, and a few lanterns from the auberge. Six musicians in their twenties, wearing jeans and loosely wrapped indigo turbans, played violins, tom-toms, tambourines, and a lute. The women wore jet black haiks with geometric splashes of orange, yellow, red, and purple embroidery tied over their caftans. The designs on the haiks serve as crests for many tribes and, when combined with the head coverings, can identify a person's specific community. Some of the dancers wore black headscarves decorated with borders of silver coins. Others had black or red scarves edged with brightly colored puffs of yarn. The women sang and danced through a rousing repertoire of traditional fireside chants, including prayers for rain, odes to the Sahara, and Moroccan folk music. They kicked up the sand with their bare feet, twirled in circles, landed on their knees,

Opposite page: *Haiks* are often draped over the body, as in this 1893 sketch of a Moroccan Berber (top) and integrated into traditional Berber dances (bottom). This page: A *real* wedding procession in Erfoud, Morocco (top) and a reenactment in Matmata, Tunisia (bottom).

A Tunisian Berber in the early 1900s.

bent over backwards, and flung their arms and hips to the rhythm of the band. As they danced, the coins on their scarves clapped like miniature cymbals. The yarn balls gyrated wildly with every dip and turn of their heads.

The party lasted until an hour before dawn. Just enough time to go rent a camel, ride it to the peak of a sand dune, and lie down and watch the sun rise.

.   .   .

For the rest of my trip, I visited Berber homes. Such visits could only be negotiated between men, so each time, my guide would approach the man of the house.

This is how I met Aisha, a forty-four-year-old mother of five who lives in the town of Tinejdad. Like other women I met, Aisha keeps her traditional clothes stored away for special occasions. Her most precious tassfifts are stored in white linen cloth inside a cardboard box, which she keeps on the back of the top shelf of her closet. She opened the cloth and revealed the white lace veil she wore on her wedding day when she was fifteen years old, a gorgeous silk purple and copper-colored scarf with purple and white tassels, and a long, diaphanous green scarf with small silver sequins.

In the town of Boumaine du Dades, I met Fatima, a thin, feisty woman with sunken cheeks and an assertive smile. She walked me through the scarves in a local shop, then, because the shop was so small, we stepped into the parking lot overlooking the valley and she demonstrated how her tribe would put them together. She layered three soft cotton scarves—one yellow, one red, and one orange, each trimmed with the now familiar yarn puffs—on my head so that the mini-tassels bounced over my hairline. She then placed a black cotton scarf on top so that its rim of loose thread dangled across my forehead and around to the back of my neck. She secured a haik over my shoulders with silver *fibules,* or traditional brooches. As I stood there under the sun in all that fabric, I realized I'd gotten used to the heat. So much so, that by the time I had to leave the desert, I was able to sit up in the car and even do some of the driving. I still didn't put my socks and shoes on, though.

Intricately crafted silver fibules from Merzouga, southern Morocco.

One week and 4,000 miles later, I was surrounded by a completely different band of Berbers. A teenage marching band, to be precise. It was the annual Festival of Matmata, a tiny community south of Tunis made famous in the 1977 film *Star Wars,* in which it provided the backdrop for the hot, arid home planet of Luke Skywalker. The all-girl teenage band was just one of a dozen acts that performed on an open dirt field near the main road. Other performances included reenactments of Berber customs, such as weddings, hand-to-hand combat, and horseback riding, as well as circus-style crowd-pleasers, such as men swallowing live scorpions.

My attention focused on a little girl about eight years old. She was fenced in behind long, gold chains that draped in layers around her neck and head. She wore a shiny fuchsia dress that dragged in the sand and had yards of bright orange and burgundy striped fabric folded and draped over her from her head to her feet. She was part of the mock wedding ceremony. In attendance with her were another little girl and half a dozen women. The women wore shiny blue and pink dresses, similar layers

Men from Mareth, a town east of
Matmata, Tunisia.

of gold, and equally long yards of bright red, purple, and orange fabric that also draped over their heads. Like the Berbers of Morocco, most Tunisian Berbers are Muslim and believe that women should be covered. What's different is their style. Many Tunisian Berbers border their scarves with larger silver discs than the ones used in Morocco, and their scarves are made of longer, bulkier fabrics with bold stripes and sequins.

The men looked drab by comparison. Their head coverings were functional. To help protect them from the heat and dust, they covered their heads with thin, cream-colored wrappers, tossing one end over their shoulders to hold them in place. Some

A drawing of various Berber tribes in their traditional costumes.

A Matmata man and his grandson outside their troglodyte.

had made turbans out of imported *shmaghs,* or checked squares of cotton fabric. They had none of the glitz of the women's coverings.

The Matmata festival lasted all day. By sunset, it was winding down. Those who had traveled long distances migrated to the cafes of New Matmata. The locals returned to their homes, underground caverns called "troglodytes." I was invited to visit with one family, whose troglodyte was at the bottom of a wide crater shared by one or two other families. After descending a long, narrow ladder, I was introduced to an old man wearing a bulbous gray and white turban. It was the first men's turban I'd seen in the country, and my translator said that the look, as well as the old man, was unique. Large turbans in the region are largely identified with nomads and Sudanese Muslims who migrate to Tunisia. Although the old man wasn't Sudanese, my translator explained that he preferred wearing turbans to other head coverings.

I would have liked to go to the Sudan, where most mainstream Sudanese men wear distinctive white turbans. Unfortunately, I was denied an entry visa before I left the States. I still had a chance to go when I met a woman from the Sudan who offered to sneak me across the border. Nervous about all the ways an adventure like that could go wrong, I decided instead to take a train and ferry over to Djerba, a tiny island in the Gulf of Gabes. No turbans and few headscarves, but lots of sun and sand. I stayed for a few days, then made preparations to go southwest to Mali.

The Sahel
(Mali and Niger)

On one road alone, I saw thirty men in voluminous turbans. I was in headwrap heaven. Geographically, of course, I was in central Mali, on a bumpy, sun-baked stretch of cemented sand and dirt between the banks of the Niger River and a paved highway that leads south to the town of Mopti. I'd just come from the famed city of Timbuktu, crossing the Niger on a *pirogue*, a canoe-type boat. This was the heart of the Sahel, just south of the Sahara and north of the West African savanna. The landscape on either side was flat and dry, spotted with dried shrubs and bushes for as far as the eye could see.

The men along the road were nomads. As traders and herders, their ancestors once traveled in camel caravans, using the sun to tell time and the stars, sand dunes, and large stones to guide their way. (Travelers passing by a stone would pick it up and place it back in the same spot to keep it from being covered by the shifting sand.) Today, more than a few have abandoned the old ways for trucks, road maps, and wristwatches. Even so, they still dress in much the same manner as their forefathers: billowy robes, flat, flexible shoes, and large, protective turbans. Their turbans range in color from gumball pink to coal black and are usually created from five to seven yards of light, breathable cotton. Each is looped around, up, and over in a way that reflects the wearer's tribe, his status within that tribe, and his individuality.

The oversized robes of the men I saw flapped like sails in the hot, dry wind. Their shoes were worn to the ground and

Previous spread: Turban styles worn in (left to right) Koura, Mopti, Niamey, and Sarafere. This page: Nomads in Timbuktu (left) and north of Niamey (right).

filthy from sand. Yet they marched on, carrying walking sticks, leather whips, and thin, rolled-up prayer mats. One man, mounted on a camel, wore a faded black turban with one of its layers pulled over his nose and mouth. Three men resting in a sliver of shade provided by a small bush wore wide, saucer-like, dark green, indigo, and burgundy turbans. A young boy tending an unruly herd of goats was wearing a light blue turban with twisted ends that was twice as big as his own head.

From Mauritania to Chad, turbans are invaluable for a variety of practical, spiritual, and social reasons. A turban wrapped with a wide base acts like a visor, protecting men from the sun and helping them to maintain their body temperature. By leaving one end of the fabric to hang loose outside of the turban, a man can quickly cover his ears, nose, and mouth. This is particularly important during the Harmattan, the Sahel's dry, windy season, when the dust irritates people's throats and nasal passages so much that outbreaks of meningitis are common.

The Tuareg, one of the largest nomadic tribes in Northwest Africa, live in the northernmost reaches of the Sahel. One Tuareg group, called the Blue Men, get their nickname from the bluish residue of their indigo-dyed fabrics that, over time, tints their skin. Like most people in the Sahel, the Blue Men are devout Muslims, but they also have strong traditional beliefs that preexist their embrace of Islam. One such belief is that evil spirits can enter a man's body through his orifices. To shield themselves, the Blue Men wrap their turbans so that the fabric covers their ears, mouth, and nose. They also believe that turbans help conceal their thoughts from their enemies.

Some Tuareg men consider it shameful to show their face in front of their in-laws, especially women. When they eat in front of their relatives, they keep their faces covered and pull part of the fabric away from their mouths to take a bite, then quickly replace it while they chew and talk.

The Soninke and Tuareg peoples consider it improper for a man to be seen in public without his turban, and removing another man's turban is the ultimate insult.

Turbans wrapped below the chin allow men to cover their nose and mouth – important protection from dust storms, whether walking the streets of Niamey (above) or riding down the Niger River near Mopti (below).

"It's so serious," said a young man in Niger, whose father worked in politics until the mid-1980s, "that, in 1988, when Niger was having civil unrest, soldiers demanded that prisoners remove their turbans, and the prisoners refused. They said they would rather die than remove their turbans." After thinking some more about the subject, the young man smiled and said, "But you know, a man refusing to remove his turban is no fool. When he goes to court, he can't be identified because no one has seen his face. Within the same tribe, people of course know one person from the next. But me, I can only tell what tribe a man comes from. It's hard to know what he looks like."

Men of the Wodaabe tribe, a nomadic group in the southern and western parts of Niger, regularly leave their silky, wavy hair loose or keep it in braids. But during their melodious, high-pitched prayer chants for rain, a good harvest, or love, they wear neatly wrapped white or black cotton turbans decorated with brass plates, woven leather straps, and ostrich plumes.

Throughout the Sahel, a man's status within his tribe is closely identified with the way he wraps his turban and wears his clothes. Tribal chiefs normally use two, three, or even four more yards of fabric than other men do, and they tend to use a

Above: Wodaabe men in Niamey, Niger perform a ritual chant for visitors.
Below: A typical rural Sahelian village in northern Mali.

better grade of fabric. Some chiefs, such as those of the Hausa in southern Niger, wrap muslin and linen around red fezes. Other chiefs and emirs (Islamic religious leaders) wear turbans made from strips of an expensive, gauze-like cotton textile known as *kura*. Hausa soldiers and guards are easily recognized by the thick, red turbans they wear. In the strict caste system of the Tuaregs, the quality and length of a man's turban, as well as the cost of his robes, help distinguish what caste he belongs to.

Most young boys in the Sahel begin wearing turbans before they learn to make their first pot of tea. In some tribes, however, boys have to be formally accepted into manhood first. Among some northern Sahelian tribes, this is done after a daylong ceremony of songs, music, and prayers from the tribe elders.

Women in the Sahel also cover their heads. The hot, arid climate has always made it necessary for them to protect themselves from the sun, wind, and evening cool. In the eighth century, however, the arrival of Islam introduced the concept of women covering their heads to preserve their modesty. In Mauritania, many women shroud themselves underneath large fabrics. In Mali, Niger, and Chad, most women wear turbans. On the small island of Kakol Daga, in the Niger River in central Mali, Bozo women wear small, simple head ties made from squares of colorful wax cotton fabric, which they most often tie with a single knot in the front. Before the Bozo converted to Islam, explained one elder, they wore decorative headbands: Young women wore blue and white checked strips of cotton around their head, older women wore solid white strips. "The old ties," said a young woman holding up a tattered piece of the blue and white checked fabric, "weren't good enough. They left too much hair exposed."

Women in the capital cities of Bamako and Niamey add a bit of style to their turbans. "We're more fashionable," explained a Bamakois woman who was shopping for new fabric. In the world of turbans, more fashionable means more elaborate, which means more folds, tucks, and other nuances. In Bamako and Niamey, Muslim women tend to set themselves apart by draping a second loose scarf over their turbans when they go outside. "This style has

A Bozo woman from Kakol Daga, Mali. Her earrings are made of cast iron wrapped in orange and red decorative thread. They are secured with a wire headband (partially hidden under her turban) to keep from weighing down her earlobes.

only been popular for the last few decades," explained a woman in Niamey. "We don't wear it all the time. Sometimes, we just put the scarf around our shoulders so it will be nearby in case we want to put it on."

Before I left the Sahel, I spent an afternoon with a Tuareg man who worked in Niamey. Putting aside his bag of roasted crickets, he talked about his coming-of-age ceremony. "I was fourteen years old," he said. "I was part of a group of other boys who'd all reached puberty together. We sat in a circle and sang songs. The elders told us how to be good men. It lasted until almost sunset, and when it was over, we were

Studio photographs such as the ones on this spread by Malick Sidibe (opposite page), and Seydou Keita were popular in Bamako in the 1950s and 1960s. They were often sent as postcards to relatives.

given new clothes, and fabric for our first turbans. Then we visited all the homes in the village and ate the food women had prepared for us. It was wonderful. After that, we were expected to wear our turbans every day. I left the desert ten years ago. In Niamey, I hardly ever wear a turban. It's not appropriate for work. But when I go home, I have to put one on. I cannot return home dressed like this," he said, pointing to his faded jeans and dark blue T-shirt. "This would never be accepted in the desert."

West Africa

(Senegal, Côte d'Ivoire, Ghana, Benin, and Nigeria)

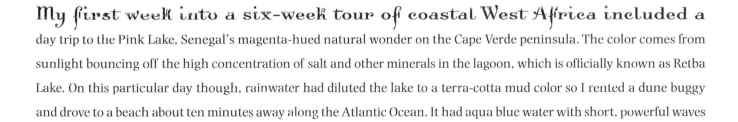

My first week into a six-week tour of coastal West Africa included a day trip to the Pink Lake, Senegal's magenta-hued natural wonder on the Cape Verde peninsula. The color comes from sunlight bouncing off the high concentration of salt and other minerals in the lagoon, which is officially known as Retba Lake. On this particular day though, rainwater had diluted the lake to a terra-cotta mud color so I rented a dune buggy and drove to a beach about ten minutes away along the Atlantic Ocean. It had aqua blue water with short, powerful waves of frothy white foam, and sand the color of cashew nuts that stretched up and down as far as the eye could see.

Up until then, I thought I knew Africa. Not all of it, of course, but many of the things that make Africa unique, such as wooden masks with decorative carvings, baobab trees with trunks as big as two football players, saucy meals like *chem-a-jem*, a tangy fish and onion dish served over rice, and clothes so colorful with patterns so wild that a walk down any street feels like being spun inside a giant kaleidoscope. That beach was the first of many surprises in the six weeks I toured coastal West Africa. With stops in Côte d'Ivoire, Ghana, Benin, and Nigeria, I discovered I had much to learn about the region's art, landscape, cuisine, and clothes.

Concerning the clothes, the first thing I needed to learn was what to buy and how. "Wax" is West Africa's most popular fabric. It is a boldly decorated cotton that is almost entirely responsible for the dizzying assortment of colors and pat-

Page 18 : An Igbo woman in Abuja, Nigeria wears a gélé made from hayes fabric. Page 19, left: These Wolof and Peuhl ladies in Dakar prefer wax head-wraps and lace headties. Right: A Queen Mother in rural Ghana dresses in ceremonial white.
This page: A matriarch wears traditional dress in Ghana's Upper Volta region.

terns seen on West African streets. Inspired by Indonesian batik and originally made and sold by the Dutch, wax is emblazoned with whimsical patterns of abstract shapes ranging from angular geometric configurations to undulating amoeba-like blobs. Produced through a process that involves applying wax to long strips of fabric before dyeing, it is spectacular in its profusion of color, a deeply saturated Pantone of bright yellow, red, purple, blue, orange, and green. (The Rolls-Royce of wax is still printed in the Netherlands.) Other popular fabrics are less aggressive but just as bright, such as the tie-dyed brocades and the solid hues of African lace.

The clothes are so lively and wild in West Africa that it's hard to believe they were not always this bright and colorful. But original dyeing techniques among many tribes, such as the Wolof and the Serai, were said to have generated bland, lifeless colors. In fact, eighteenth-century French traders, who traveled along the Senegal and Gambia rivers in search of tradable goods (everything from gum arabic to women), complained that local fabrics were boring and unfit for foreign export. And the Yoruba people in what is now western Nigeria have only a few words for color in their native tongue, such as *fufon* for light (or white) and *dudu* for dark (indigo or black). Some tribes, of course, such as the Ashanti and the Fon in what are now parts of Ghana and Benin, respectively, have long harvested rich yellow, red, and blue dyes from a variety of local plants to dye cotton and make clothes. But trade between tribes was rare. Fabric was considered a mark of tribal identity, and so were the headwraps and clothes that were made with it.

But even as the French traders made their way through Senegambia, change was already in the works. Links between Senegal and North Africa were established by the tenth century, the Tukolor people converted to Islam in the eleventh century, other ethnic groups converted in the centuries before and after, and the Portuguese introduced European culture in the fifteenth century. These influences, along with the rise of new cultures (the Ghana Empire around 1000, the complex kingdoms of the Yoruba people beginning in the eleventh century, and the Mali Empire in the thirteenth century), introduced new religions, lifestyles, dyeing techniques, fabric, and fashions. Over the centuries, headwraps evolved from a random utility cloth used to shield women from the climate to an increasingly important Islamic, and later Christian, religious statement, as well as a socially important fashion statement. The Yoruba were among the first to wear headwraps as adornments. The idea spread, so that by the 1400s, headwraps of some kind were a firm part of many West African cultures. By the 1600s, European fashions, including hats, bonnets, and headscarves, did much to spark the current trend of developing new, trendy headwrap styles.

Called a *foulard* in French, a *mussor* in Wolof, a *gélé* in Yoruba, and countless other names among hundreds of other tribes, headwraps for some people were originally no more than strips of animal hide tied over the forehead. "When men returned from their hunts, women cleaned the animals and used the skin as headbands," explained an elder woman in Rufisque, a town south of Dakar. "Before fabric was affordable,

Traditional tribal styles worn by young women in Congo (top) and rural Ghana (bottom).

Muslim Hausa women in Accra, including Alhajia Azumi Ibrahim (bottom), my hostess in Ghana.

chiefs and their wives were the only ones who owned enough to spare."

It didn't take long for fabric to become accessible, thanks in large part to wax, a neutral, nontribal-specific cloth that was embraced by many West African cultures. These days, everything from the loose-fitting pants and matching tunics worn by men, to baby harnesses tightly wrapped and knotted around women's backs, to women's *boubous* (long dresses), *bubas* (long-sleeved, waist-length tops, worn with matching *wrappers*, or wraparound skirts), and headwraps are made of the fabric.

Turbans were originally tribal specific. The Yoruba had their own style and the Igbo had theirs. And in Senegal in the eighteenth and nineteenth centuries, a class of women known as *signares* had their own style, as well. Named after the Portuguese word for "ladies" *(senhoras)*, signares were the mulatto descendants of Portuguese or French colonists and local women. Generally considered French citizens, they formed common-law marriages with the Europeans and lived in luxury with hand-maidens and slaves of their own. Their unique style of dress included towering head-dresses modeled off the conical *hennin* hats of Europe. Made with madras fabric imported from India, or silk from France, their tubular and cone-shaped turbans were often formed around a mold of stiff paper and reached a peak as high as two to three feet above their heads.

Religious beliefs and customs play an important role in how headwraps are worn. "Headwraps have always been important in northern Ghana because they are Muslims," explained a college graduate in Accra. "When I was young, Christians in Ghana never wore headwraps, and people in the south never wore gélés," she said. Additionally, to identify themselves as Muslim, many women throughout West Africa, like those in Bamako and Niamey, drape a thin, second scarf over their tur-bans. A general rule regarding headwraps is that they are never worn with Western clothes, "unless, of course, the clothes were tailored with African fabrics," the woman in Accra said.

And then there is fashion. As early as the 1600s, some ethnic groups were creating stylish headwraps with often small amounts of fabric. By the early 1900s, creating new headwrap styles had become an art. Headwraps resembling everything from pill-box hats to angelic halos and cubist sculptures were invented all the time by cleverly adding or removing a knot, pulling out a point, tilting the wrap to one side, tucking in the center, or tucking under the outside rim. The sides could be puffed out, angled,

Igbo women outside St. Mary's Anglican Church in eastern Nigeria.

or elongated. Parts of the cloth could be twisted, rolled, wrapped, or tucked. Props such as empty twenty-ounce tomato cans, stiff cardboard, and tufts of wool or fake hair could be put to use, as well as stickpins and bobby pins.

A lot of new styles are inspired by events in society, such as a new currency or the national soccer team winning a tournament. When Nigeria switched from driving on the right-hand side of the road to the left, a new turban called the "the right-hand drive" was created and became an instant success. Other styles are inspired by world trends. In the 1940s, the Yoruba created a style called *ahe-keo,* or "skyward," which had two points sticking straight up, mimicking the high-rise buildings in the West. Other styles were inspired by helicopters, Concorde planes, and Mercedes-Benz cars. When a prominent woman invents a style, it is usually named after her. This was the case with the *Konadu,* named after the wife of Ghana's fourth president, and the *Madeleine,* after Marie Madeleine Valfroy Diallo, a Senegalese actress.

The 1950s "Nguuka" style in Senegal.

Igbo women at a wedding in Lagos wear matching colors and fabrics to indicate their special relationship to the bride.

I met Marie Madeleine at her home in St. Louis, northern Senegal. While having coffee in her living room, which was decorated with a portrait of her painted by her husband, the Senegalese artist Jacob Yakouba, she explained the origin of her signature style. One morning in the early 1990s, she stood in front of a mirror with two yards of fabric at the nape of her neck. Rather than do something elaborate, she simply flipped the two ends over her head. The left end went to the right side, the right end went to the left. And she was done. For months, Marie Madeleine wore that style at all of her public appearances, and she continued to wear it occasionally for years after that. It quickly caught on in Senegal and the Gambia and for a time was the most popular style around.

Most new styles only stay in fashion for a few months. To keep up, women occasionally pay a professional stylist to help them out. Maman Téte, a stern-faced, heavy-set woman in Cotonou, is one of only two professional stylists in southern Benin. For the past twenty years, she has created elaborate, centerpiece-type headwraps in the style of the Yoruba-designed gélés. A weather-worn, painted aluminum sign led me to her shop. She prefers hayes, a stiff, often metallic fabric, and wax, and practices on a foam mannequin to avoid accidentally sticking a paying customer with a straight pin.

As for me, learning to tie the most popular styles in each country was more than I could handle. It was hard enough for me to just keep my boubou on my shoulders and the sleeves of my buba from falling into my food. To alleviate the pressure, I was content to wear hassle-free braids and my all-too-familiar Western-style clothes. This system worked fine until I got to Nigeria. There, I stayed with an Igbo chief and his family. The mother, Mrs. Igwe, frowned at my braids (hairstyles, as it turns out, are as regionally specific as headwraps) and the father, Chief Sir Johnson Igwe, shook his head at my clothes. Between the two of them, I was shamed into making a greater effort at wearing African clothes.

My forays into headwrap tying were pitiful. On most days, I could get by after some struggle, and the family would let me go out with just disgusted shakes of their heads. But everything had to be in order on the day of their daughter's wedding. Chinelo Igwe, a twenty-eight-year-old computer technician in Lagos, was about to marry Ifeanyi Gordian Nweke for the second time in as many months. This was Chinelo's Christian wedding, where she'd be married in the eyes of God. (Her first nuptials, which followed the traditions of her people, were held in a separate ceremony before I arrived.)

Weddings bring out the best in West African women's headwraps. It was made clear that while I may have been an outsider, there was no excuse for me to look like one. So, to match my lavender lace buba—tailored especially for me the day before—I had a lavender and royal purple headwrap made of *aso-oke* (a woven textile invented by the Yoruba) and a matching sash. The outfit was gorgeous. Putting it on and getting it to look as good as the other women's, however, was impossible. I fumbled around for an hour until, in the spirit of sisterhood, I got much needed assistance. One woman redid the skirt (who knew there was a "right" way to wrap a wraparound skirt?), another tied the sash around my waist (the knot had to be just so), and a third sat me down and tackled the headwrap. In less time than it took me to learn to eat

Above: Igbo women in Awka Etiti, Nigeria, including my hostess, Nwayibuife Igwe (bottom). Left: Maman Téte works on a headwrap.

Abuakar Wazidi, *sawki* of Kubwa village, near Abuja, Nigeria, wraps his signature turban around a red fez.

fufu—a thick, starchy white porridge that's supposed to be balled up in your hand, placed on the back of your tongue near the throat, and swallowed whole—I was not only perfectly presentable for the wedding but looked as good as any woman in Lagos. And in the world of traditional West African fashion, how you look is all that matters.

For women anyway.

What often matters with men is the size and color of the turban. Most men in coastal West Africa wear flat-topped, brimless caps with their traditional clothes. But in northern and central Nigeria, turbans are more common, particularly among tribal chiefs. Gorki, Hausa, and Fulani chiefs, for example, often wear large, voluminous white or yellow turbans, and their guards and soldiers tend to wear red ones. "Most of the northern tribes are Muslim, and their chiefs try to Islamicize everything," explained a Hausa woman from northern Nigeria. "They want to be spiritual leaders and cultural leaders. The turban helps bridge the two, and it is the only way to differentiate chiefs from ordinary men on the street."

I visited chiefs in three villages in central Nigeria. The small village of Kubwa, outside of Abuja, is a poor community but its chief, or *sawki*, commands a great deal of respect. In order to talk to him, I had to be introduced and announced, and then I was seated on the ground just inside a mud-brick and straw shelter reserved for tribal matters. Within seconds, a group of officers dressed in jeans and old button-down shirts filed in and sat on the floor opposite me. Finally, sawki Abuaker Wazidi entered and sat in a wooden armchair with a worn cushion. He wore a crisp white robe with dark blue embroidery and a cream-colored turban wrapped around a red fez. One end of the fabric covered his neck, looped under his chin, and was left as a tail to hang down his back. His eldest daughter stood beside him and translated. The sawki, a thin man in his fifties with jet-black skin and a low, deep voice, explained that he alone is allowed to wear the headdress, which has been a symbol of his office for generations. He said that as a child he was never allowed to play with his father's turban, and in 1998 when his father died and it was his turn, it took him months to learn to tie it properly. Aside from the teachers who originally instructed him, no one is allowed to touch the felt cap or the cloth, not even his wives.

While the chief had me in his presence, he took the opportunity to learn some things from me. He'd heard that in America, a man can only have one wife, and that a woman can divorce her husband and take half of his wealth. When I confirmed the rumor, the men in the room gasped, and I detected a sly smirk on the daughter's face. Wazidi smiled and said that things are very different between our two countries, and that it's good for people to travel and share their stories.

There were many other stories that I shared and learned, some with the wife of Nigeria's vice president, some with teenage girls thinking about going to college. Every conversation that began about headwraps ended with something about a traditional aspect of Africa and its people. It was a long six weeks before I finished, but in many ways, it wasn't nearly long enough.

South Africa

For people who know nothing about the ethnic groups in South Africa, the Khaya Lendaba Cultural Village puts on one hell of a show. Here, a professional dance troupe of Xhosa, Zulu, and Sutu men and women make their way from stage to hut to open field as they reenact rituals, ceremonies, stick fights, and daily chores traditional to their peoples. Starting with a rousing performance on a small stage at the entrance to the village, their show is free for everyone who pays to enter the Shamwari Game Reserve. (On the reserve, the closest I got to any of the big game advertised was a mound of rhinoceros dung, and if it hadn't been for the dance troupe, the whole day would have been a waste—no pun intended.)

The men wore strips of sheep's wool around their shins, flaps of animal hide around their waists, and small black scarves on their heads. But it was the women who looked really interesting. They dressed according to marital status. Young, unmarried girls wore short orange, white, red, or black skirts with either matching halter tops or bare breasts and simple, close-fitting head ties with single knots in the front or back. Engaged women wore loose-fitting tunics and skirts that reached their knees, either in cotton or animal hide, depending on their ethnic group. Married women wore dresses or skirts that reached their ankles, matching tunics, shawls, and aprons. The headgear was varied. Zulu women wore hats that were wide and flat at the top, then curved inward and down to a fitted, brimless bottom. Sutu women wore hats that

Members of the Khaya Lendaba dance troupe perform a cultural show. The women's short skirts indicate that they are still single.

were wide at the bottom and angled up to a center point at the top. Xhosa women wore headwraps.

The show is a simplified version of the many South African tribal traditions. There are dozens of Xhosa groups, including the Xhosa tribe, which has two major divisions, and the many tribes of other Xhosa-speaking peoples. They have numerous headwear styles, ranging from beaded headbands to layers of red clay smeared in the hair. The styles are sometimes tribal specific and clearly identify a woman's marital status. A Xhosa woman always wears some form of headdress out of respect for the male head of the family, whether he is her father or her husband. Many also have specific headdresses to show respect for their boyfriends and fiancés. Though styles vary widely from tribe to tribe, in general headwraps among the Xhosa are made with one or two pieces of fabric and usually have a corner of the fabric sticking out on one side, in the back, or at the top. They are usually made from the same fabric as the women's clothes, which are commonly thick cotton textiles with bold, solid colors such as red, orange, black, or white adorned at the edges with thin horizontal white or black lines.

Not all headwraps are turbans. Single girls sometimes wear headbands or simple

head ties. One example of a head tie for unmarried girls is a single square of fabric placed over her head so that one corner lies flat over one ear; the fabric is then pulled tight into a decorative knot over the other ear, and the excess is left to hang down the side. Another head tie is crafted so that a corner of the fabric sticks above the center of a woman's head; an outer fold is pulled over the sides of her head from the nape of her neck to the front, then tied in a knot above her forehead.

On her wedding day, a bride wears a different headwrap. Among the Fingo people, a Xhosa-speaking tribe, the rim of a bride's headwrap partially covers her eyes in a sign of respect for the groom and the future father-in-law. Young wives who haven't had their first child are also distinguished by a specific style. For instance, Bomvana wives without children adorn their turbans with orange pom-poms that are attached to a strip of cloth. The full-blown turbans of married women with children can be extremely large and are often created from two or more pieces of fabric. Some styles are tubular or bowl shaped, with rounded sides, simple folds at the top, and decorative corners protruding down the forehead or off to one side. Others are more bulbous and abstract, with the ends and corners jutting out in every direction. Still others form voluminous peaks that rise from the back, slope down the front, and have a second, narrow strip of cloth wrapped around the width.

Xhosa women wear different headwraps throughout their traditional territories. Page 28: A performer in the Khaya Lendaba cultural show plays the role of the Great Wife. Page 29 and above, right: Women and children in the Wild Coast, Eastern Cape Province. Above, left: Two women near Lesotho.

Known as *umbaco*, these traditional Xhosa garments have been around at least since the 1800s. Before then, most Xhosa garments were made from ox hide and animal pelts. Traditional dress is rarely seen in South Africa's large cities, particularly outside of each ethnic group's territory, which for the Xhosa loosely extends throughout the Eastern Cape between Port Elizabeth and Port Edward. Even in rural areas, traditional dress has been less common since the 1970s, generally because Western clothes are cheaper. Most women wear Western-style clothes and headscarves, saving their traditional clothes for special occasions such as weddings, funerals, and coming-of-age ceremonies. As in West Africa, traditional Xhosa headwraps are rarely worn with Western clothes, although rural women still wear headwraps of some sort to show respect for the men in their lives.

As a special favor to me, two women in the village of Mgwali put on traditional turbans with their everyday clothes. Their bulky, six-inch-high orange and bright pink turbans with large, drooping corners made it clear that they were married and had children. In the same village, a small community of about two dozen thatched-roof huts at the end of a long, gravel road amidst low, rolling hills, I met a *sangoma*, Swazi for a traditional healer. She invited me into her home, which was dimly lit. A single lightbulb, several ears of corn, and an empty calabash hung from the ceiling. The walls were covered with the hides of springboks, goats, squirrels, foxes, and other animals. The light gray floor was made from hardened cow dung. Lining the floor edges

Xhosa women wear their turbans with the ends tucked in (above) or hanging loose (left).

A *sangoma* in her *Mgwali*.

were an assortment of herbs, roots, and animal bones as well as bottles of vodka, rum, and whiskey. As instructed, I took off my shoes and sat on the floor, then asked the sangoma about her turban.

She was seventy-two years old and spoke in a guttural whisper. She wore a sleeveless white top, a long white skirt, and navy blue sneakers with no laces. She was adorned with bracelets around her wrist and elbows and a white choker around her neck that had long strands of yarn and beads hanging from it. Her white turban was a thick terry-cloth

Right: Pipe smoking is a luxury of older women. Women's pipes often have long stems. This pipe-smoker in Eastern Cape Province wears a bulbous headwrap typical of the region. Below: Women in the Transkeii often wear smooth, rounded headwraps.

towel. She said that as a mother and a wife, she wears a headwrap out of respect and tradition. As a sangoma, she wears white as a symbol of purity. Other sangomas, both men and women, also wear white turbans, ribbons, and beaded headdresses.

In an even smaller community east of the Great Kei River, near the birthplace of Nelson Mandela, who is Thembu, is a Xhosa-speaking tribe. I arrived just in time for a *braai,* or barbecue over an open fire. Everyone in the village had gathered in honor of a sixteen-year-old *amakrwala,* a young man who had just completed his circumcision rite. He'd been in seclusion in the bush with other initiates, learning the traditional laws of conduct and ways to honor his ancestral spirits. Most of the other amakrwalas had returned a few days earlier. For a reason that was not explained to me, he had remained behind and returned alone. While children played with sticks along the dirt road, the men lounged in a large *krall*, or animal corral, which is generally forbidden to women. They had spent the morning slaughtering sheep and cooking the meat. Smoke from the pit, which used cow dung for coal, created a thick fog. The women were gathered around their own, smaller fire a few feet from the krall. They were preparing bread, side dishes, and the sheep entrails. They wore their comfortable, everyday clothes: elastic skirts, long-sleeved tops, sweaters, and simple head ties with single knots in the back. "Normally, for such a celebration the women would wear their traditional clothes," explained my guide. "But they just lost someone important in the village and are exhausted from the funeral. Right now, everyone is sad. They want to make the amakrwala feel welcome, but want to do it in their everyday clothes."

When the guest of honor was spotted walking across the *veld*, or open plateau, toward us, he wore a small black turban and clung to a forest green blanket that was draped around his shoulders. All of his old clothes had been taken away, and he was about to receive new clothes in which to enter the world as a man. He was greeted with love, invited to assume his place in the krall, and given his pick of the meat. He was still in his blanket and turban when I left.

I was back in Port Elizabeth when I met four high school girls in traditional Xhosa dress. They'd just left a school dance where everyone wore traditional clothes, and they were thrilled at how it turned out. "We helped organize the dance. We're Christians and people always say that we've turned our backs on our Xhosa heritage. That's not true. We love that we are Xhosa. We wanted to do this to show that we can be both—Christian and Xhosa." Their clothes were similar to the ones worn by the Khaya Lendaba dance troupe: short skirts in solid colors with horizontal stripes along the edges. Their turbans, however, weren't the simple head ties traditionally worn by single girls. "Yeah, our turbans are wrong, but these look nicer," they said and smiled.

Women near Mvebo prepare the side dishes at a *braai*. They are dressed in Western clothes, which are more affordable and easier to maintain than their traditional garments, but they still wear headwraps.

Kenya

After three months of nonstop research, I felt I was due for a break, which is what brought me to Nairobi. Kenya was never supposed to be part of this book. Its many ethnic groups, such as the Kalenjin, Masai, Kikuyu, and Samburu, prefer beaded, wooden, or feather headdresses to headwraps, if they wear headdresses at all. When I added the trip to my itinerary, my plan was to just rest. I looked forward to going on a safari or two, maybe seeing some of the big game that had eluded me in South Africa. But as soon as I landed in Nairobi, I learned that headscarves did exist in the country, and my trip of leisure was put on hold.

Two types of all-engulfing headscarves cover women from head to toe in two distinctly different parts of Kenya: the *chador* is worn in Eastleigh, and the *buibui* is worn on the island of Lamu. These are both Muslim communities, and they observe the strictest interpretations of Islamic doctrine that I came across, at least with regard to women's clothing.

Eastleigh is one of Kenya's largest communities of Somali immigrants and refugees. It is a crowded slum on the outskirts of Nairobi with unfinished, mud-brick homes lined along a maze of nameless dirt roads. Electricity comes in spurts, and plumbing is so rare that beauticians have to fill five-gallon buckets with water from an outside spout just to wash their clients' hair.

The residents of Eastleigh keep to themselves. They speak Kiswahili like most other Kenyans, but their religious beliefs and immigrant status set them apart. They are Sunni Muslims, whereas the majority of Nairobi's population is Christian or animist. They are distrustful of outsiders, and they rarely leave their community, especially the women, who are kept hidden, in plain view, underneath yards of fabric. As they walked about in their chadors, which are more colorful than those in rural Morocco, they looked to me like giant jellybeans in the dusty maze of the two- and three-story buildings. Some women wore solid colors, often deep purples and vivid blues; others wore busy patterns, such as bright stripes and soft florals. Many women wore matching veils that hung from the bridge of the nose down over the face, leaving an inch or so of space for their eyes. Others wore a full-frontal *burqa*, a fabric, leather, or plastic veil that completely covers the face, with the exception of small holes or a piece of mesh around the eyes. Some burqas come in the form of large coverings that shroud the entire body, except for the eyes and the tips of the fingers. The few who didn't wear veils or burqas used their hands to lift a portion of their chador over their faces.

I stayed in Eastleigh for three days trying to make connections with women. The first group of women who stopped and talked with me were suspicious at first. "Americans don't understand the chador," they chimed. They thought I was there to judge their Islamic beliefs. My guide, a Kikuyu man in his forties, convinced them I was different, and after a while, they relaxed. I couldn't tell how old the women were because of their veils. They said they liked their chadors and that being covered made them feel safe and protected when walking in the neighborhood. They also explained that it is important for good Muslims to follow the words of Allah and the Prophet Muhammad.

As we talked, four men started yelling at the women from a block away, "Why are you talking to those people?" The men had been sitting on the hood of an old car parked on the side of the road. They looked like they were ready to fight. I couldn't see the women's faces, but from the opening of their veils, I could see the fear in their eyes. The men stormed over to where we stood. They were all shorter than the women they were fussing at. The women tried to explain, but the men were too furious to listen. They stood neck to chador with the women and screamed, "What business is it of hers?" and other things my guide refused to translate. The men yelled so loudly, and with such anger, that the women bowed their heads, apologized to the men, and walked away without ever looking at me again. Within seconds, they

Previous spread and opposite page: The women wrapped in *chadors* are Somalian immigrants who live in Eastleigh, a suburb of Nairobi. The men in white turbans are from a Christian sect known as the Akorinos.

faded into the crowded street, each woman's chador quickly blending into the sea of fabric.

I was much more discreet when I met two sisters, Sadia and Amina, and their friend, Muna. Our clandestine conversations took place in the courtyard of Sadia's home, which is hidden from the street by a mud-brick wall and narrow wooden gate. The three women, all between eighteen and twenty-two years old, talked softly, their conversation punctuated with nervous giggles. Several children ran around the courtyard and happily kept lookout for approaching men.

Women in Lamu are very concerned about having their faces covered. This woman's face veil is securely tucked into a fold of her *hijab*, but she holds it up anyway to ensure it doesn't fall.

Opposite page, top: The women of Lamu nickname their way of wearing the *buibui* the "ninja" style.
Bottom: Beautiful carved doors with thick metal bolts line the streets and passageways of Lamu.

Sadia wore a light yellow and white striped chador, her favorite, she said. It was slightly see-through, so she wore a tan pullover dress underneath. Amina had on a deep burgundy chador, and Muna wore a green one. As much as they were willing to risk talking to me, they refused to allow my guide into the courtyard. Without his translations, we relied on Sadia's limited English and the creative use of hand signals. They asked if I believed in God and wanted to know what Americans thought about their chadors. They talked about Somalia, which has a porous border with Kenya and a long history of immigrants traveling back and forth. Muna was an illegal refugee brought to the region to escape the 1990s war and chaos in Mogadishu. She was extremely concerned that the pictures I was taking would end up on a postcard and allow anyone that recognized her to know where she was, and perhaps cause them to think that she was behaving improperly.

After we chatted for a while, Sadia agreed to take me to the outdoor market where the fabric is sold. Although I was dressed modestly, I wasn't covered in a chador, which would have alerted everyone to the fact that Sadia was with an outsider. To protect us both, Amina loaned me one of her headscarves. The market was a complicated jumble of poorly lit kiosks and narrow paths. Sadia held my hand and quickly swept me past stands piled high with spices, meats, and incense. We both kept our heads down, Sadia to avoid eye contact with the men, and I to make sure I didn't trip over a pothole or the uneven rises in the path. Nine or ten shops in the rear of the market sold scarves. They were all run by women, so Sadia and other female shoppers could browse in peace. The fabric is sold by the meter and then sewn into a chador or other covering. There was a small section of "African fabric" that included wax, hayes, and tie-dyed cotton. The rest of the material was a range of polyester, cotton, silk, and wool blends in solid colors and soft patterns, such as daisies, bumblebees, stripes, and checks.

My time in Eastleigh prepared me well for Lamu, where the women wear a black all-in-one headscarf and body covering called a *buibui*. Lamu is a small island off the coast of Kenya, about 40 miles south of the Somali border. There is one motor vehicle on the entire island. Most people get around on foot (it takes less than an hour to traverse the whole island), by donkey, or in *dhows* (small wooden boats). Most men on Lamu are fishermen, although a few work in shops or dedicate their lives to studying the Qur'an. The women stay at home. Occasionally, one or two are seen scampering through the labyrinth of narrow streets to get to the market and back home. They talk to merchants from behind their veils, pointing to items carefully so that their hands remain mostly covered by fabric. They go to the movies and sit on the beach fully covered in their buibuis. They do not talk to outsiders.

To get an interview with a woman, I had to go through a man. I noticed that a lot of men hung around the northeast side of the island, near the free donkey clinic funded by the government of Saudi Arabia. I had to isolate one of them, convince him that I was nonthreatening, and get him to introduce me to a woman who would answer my questions. In the early hours of my second day there, I was introduced to Alya, a divorcée with young children and no father—in other words, someone who lives on her own and has no man around to forbid her from talking.

I met Alya in a bed and breakfast where she works. Our conversation focused on the role of women in Islam. Alya's voice was confident and engaging, almost maternal. "A good Muslim woman should . . ." is how she started each sentence. (Her English was almost perfect.) She talked about the importance of cleanliness, prayer, cooking, obeying one's husband, and obeying the Qur'an. Wearing the buibui was one of the most important ways a woman could obey the Qur'an, according to Alya, who insisted that married women, especially, should always cover their bodies and faces. She felt that young women who dress *ninja* do so only to avoid being identified when they go off to the tourist clubs, or with their boyfriends.

There are two kinds of buibui, the older style, which is a large tubular body covering with the hijab sewn onto it like a hood, and a newer, double-breasted robe version with a separate, matching hijab. Alya showed me how to properly wear the buibui, which is slipped into like a dress and adjusted to cover the face and whole body like a ninja. It can also be adjusted to expose the upper body and reveal an equally concealing blouse or other undergarment. Then, while her twelve-year-old son showed me how to play the local version of mancala, a game of strategy popular throughout Africa, she wrote down all the things I needed to remember to become a good Muslim.

Another woman I met had left Lamu to start a life in Toronto and was returning for a visit. "I have to dress traditionally when I come home, but I never wear clothes like this in Canada," she said. I also met a "commercial woman," or prostitute, in a meeting arranged by a waiter at the hotel. In discussing my interest in head coverings, the waiter reflected the same attitude of other men I had spoken with. "Women who do not care about the laws of Islam are the ones who don't cover their face," he said. "But married women must so they are not seen by other men."

Underneath the veils, most women wear makeup and style their hair in the latest

Near the dock, on the eastern edge of Lamu.

trends. "They show off to other women when their husbands are not around," said the waiter. "After all," he said, "a woman must always look her best."

Before leaving Lamu, I went to the beach with Alya's son. According to him, "A Muslim man does not love his wife if he is not jealous. It's natural that he doesn't want other men looking at her."

Back in Nairobi, I later discovered another group that wears headwraps and headscarves. It's a Christian sect of the Church of Prophets known as the Akorinos, or "Saved Ones." Three men from the Riabai Akorino Church of Prophets stood with me on a crowded sidewalk in downtown Nairobi and talked about their beliefs. Naming passages in the Bible such as Zechariah 3:5, Revelations 3:4–18, and others, the three explained that men and women should wear solid white turbans and headscarves, covering all of their hair, at all times, except when sleeping. To that end, they place a small, white cap on their children when they are eight days old. When they are three months old, children start wearing the turban. Fathers put it on their sons; mothers do the same for their daughters. As the children grow older, they are taught how to keep their hair completely hidden. Most adult women wear headscarves. Men continue to wear turbans, which they tie over a knit cap.

I planned on leaving Kenya the next day, not at all rested, but pleased with the way things had turned out. I was admittedly disappointed about not doing a safari, or something really wild like hiking up Kilimanjaro. And with only one country remaining to visit in Africa, I longed for the opportunity to go to the Sudan, the Congo, Egypt, Tanzania, and other countries where head coverings are worn. But I knew that if I only had time to visit one country, it should be Ethiopia.

Akorinos cover all of their hair and only remove their turbans at night, just before bed.

Ethiopia

I arrived in Lalibela just after sunrise on a Saturday morning. The airport is tucked in the middle of a roller coaster of lush green mountains and valleys in Ethiopia's central highlands. A mini-bus for tourists drove me to the center of town, about forty-five minutes up a steep and winding two-lane road. Dozens of villagers who live in the outlying countryside were making a similar trek by foot. Their steps were in sync with sturdy walking sticks, and they used colorful yellow and pink parasols with matching tassels to block the sun. We were all on our way to Lalibela's weekly market, the largest in the region.

Lalibela is an ancient town of stone-pitted roads and round log homes with thatched roofs. The market is set up on an open dirt field on a plateau at the edge of town. There, spaced out along a grid of nine or ten rows, vendors sit on blankets and sheets behind their wares—homegrown vegetables and herbs, dried fish, fruit, and clothes made from Ethiopia's signature gauze-like cotton. A lone vendor in a tattered head tie in the rear of the second row was selling three varieties of freshly harvested honey, including *tsadena*, a rich, white honey that many use as a heart medicine. The market attracts hundreds of local highlanders who come to weigh down their donkeys and load up their wicker baskets and clay jugs, called *gumbos*.

The market, however, isn't what makes Lalibela famous. Lalibela is famous among architects, anthropologists, and

Previous spread and this page: Ethiopian Orthodox priests from Lalibela wear small, tightly wound white turbans. For women in Lalibela, headwraps are less common but tend to be more versatile.

Orthodox Christians around the world for its many churches. It is the home of eighteen landmark structures—nearly all of which date back to the twelfth century, and eleven of which were hewn out of solid rock.

The priests wear distinctive small white turbans, called *metamaeas*. The archbishop gives each priest his first metamaea, and a handheld cross, or *meskal*, when he is ordained. The meskal is carved from an unsplit piece of strong wood, such as oak. The turban is made from a single strip of white cotton. The white, one deacon explained, represents the priest's purity.

Priests in the Ethiopian Orthodox Church have been wearing turbans since the fourth century, when Christianity became the state religion of Ethiopia. At that time, the Ethiopian church was under the leadership of the Egyptian Coptic Church, which appointed its bishops. Bishops in the Egyptian Coptic Church wear black turbans, and when the Ethiopian Orthodox Church gained its independence in the mid-1900s, its high-ranking clergymen continued to wear black turbans. They switch to white silk ones for special ceremonies.

Recounting his lessons from the Old Testament, a deacon explained that Aaron and other important figures in the Bible wore turbans. "It is important we continue their traditions," he said. Underneath their turbans, priests wear a small white hat, or skullcap, which helps keep the turban in place. Married priests leave an opening in the center of their turbans, and unmarried ones wrap their entire heads. When praying and meditating, priests shroud their faces with long, white veils.

It can take fifteen years for a young boy to become a priest and have the right to wear a white turban. While he is a young student in theology school, he wears a small, white headscarf that's wrapped in the back and tied in the front. *Debterras*, educated clergymen who are not priests, wear tall, pointed, white cotton headpieces called *timtems*. The latter term actually refers to any piece of clothing that one wraps, such as the headpiece or even a wrapped skirt.

In Lalibela, and in towns such as Aksum in the far north and Bahar Dar in the

An illustration of Palm Sunday in northern Ethiopia.

south, the Ethiopian Orthodox Church is dominant. In those communities, white turbans are generally worn only by priests. But millions of men and women wear turbans in Ethiopia, and outside of the towns mentioned, they wear any color fabric they want. The turbans of nonordained men are also called timtems. In some regions, men's timtems are tribal specific but also vary according to personal style and the length of material available. Some men, such as a young man I saw cutting sug-

In and around Bahar Dar, men wear colorful turbans to help shield them from the sun, whether walking in town (above), or chopping sugar cane in the fields (left).

arcane in a field near Bahar Dar, wrap their turbans only to cover the tops of their heads, leaving out their ears and the bottom half of their heads. Nomadic travelers, or *zellans*, make their way through the countryside in large, multicolored turbans that are loosely wound from the hairline to the nape of the neck, often leaving one end of the fabric hanging down over one shoulder.

Women's headscarves are called *shashes*, which are viewed as protectors of women's integrity. Most traditional outfits in Ethiopia are considered incomplete without a long shash, a handwoven cotton scarf with a colorful, geometric border design. Older women usually cover their whole heads. Young women often wear decorative variations of headbands that leave much of the hair uncovered. "Except when we go to church," explained a woman from the highlands who attends an Orthodox church in Lalibela. "In church, we cover our heads with a *shama*," she continued, referring to a white, muslin shawl.

Women in the large Islamic communities in the east of Ethiopia and in Addis Ababa wear hijabs as well as shashes, shamas, and other coverings. On Muslim holy days, thousands of men and women in turbans and headscarves gather outdoors to pray and worship. I was there on a return trip to Africa during Ramadan. Traffic was stopped for miles in Addis Ababa as streets were carpeted with Muslims who pros-

A basket weaver wears a narrow shash tied around her head.

trated in rows, shoulder-to-shoulder and toe-to-knee, with women and their daughters separated from men and their sons. Their headwraps were all different colors, some white with blue motifs, some floral, some striped, some solid. They stayed there for hours, kneeling on sheets, blankets, and plastic bags. "Our headscarves are part of our lives. Today is no different from how we dress every day," explained one woman, who had to carve out a spot on the sidewalk because the street was so crowded.

The Christians also gather on holy days. During Christmas, or *Genna*, hundreds of priests in freshly laundered turbans and robes gather at Bete Mariam, one of the historic churches in Lalibela. Several people described how dozens of priests stand shoulder to shoulder along the stone wall that surrounds the church, forming a human fence of devotees and a symbolic representation of God. Below, other priests stand side by side to form an even larger circle representing the

Everyday life in Bahar Dar requires a headwrap for men and women.

earth and creation. The priests above and those below bow to each other, turbans to turbans, as they chant: *Yom tewelde beza kulu alem* ("This day is born the redeemer of all the world"). "It's a beautiful thing to see," recounted one priest. "Our turbans are like a beacon—as brilliant as the sun above, and the light that comes from God. During Genna, everything is so beautiful. You should see it, so many priests together at one time."

It was fitting that my last African country should be Ethiopia, whose Christian roots bear homage to the beginning of the Christian church in Rome. I flew directly to Italy on Ethiopian Airlines and sat amidst people fluent in both Italian and Amharic. The multicultural vibe did much to help me shift gears and prepare for life on a new continent. *Dehnahunge Afrika!* and *Ciao Europa!*

Europe

Italy

I typically go four months without wearing the same outfit twice. But during my year abroad, I had to wear the same clothes once, sometimes twice, every single week. My entire wardrobe—the six outfits I wore for the first half of the year and the other six for the next—was a bland mix of monochromatic cotton and polyester rags that, by the time I reached Italy, had become a source of profound boredom and discontent. But

a week into my stay in Rome, my perspective changed. I met Sister Clare Millea, a nun in the Congregation of the Apostles of the Sacred Heart of Jesus. Sister Clare's closet is stocked with multiple sets of one single outfit: a shapeless, black, ankle-length robe with a rounded white collar. Also, where I could at least change my look by doing fun things with my hair, she kept hers pinned up and nearly covered with a black polyester veil, of which she had a collection. For the entire afternoon, as we sat at a small wooden table with a doily centerpiece in her convent's conference room, I harbored a single pleasing thought in the back of my head: At least my outfits, as measly as they are, are all different.

Sister Clare was the most friendly and helpful person I met or tried to meet in the

Catholic Church. I'd come to Italy to learn about the origins of veils in Christianity. In Africa, the history of the headwrap could be gleaned from the descendants of the very people who had invented them, but Italy's history with veils lies locked in the archives of its religious and educational institutions.

Italy's heyday of veils and other hair accessories started more than twenty centuries ago, long before the country was named Italy or Catholicism was born. Getting access to libraries, meeting the right people, and sifting through the lore put me on a kind of treasure hunt that took me through the streets of Rome and Naples and to the ruins of Pompeii. At one point, when I found myself on the Ponte Palatino, one of a dozen bridges in Rome that cross over the Tevere River, I tried to imagine summertime with the Vestal Virgins. The Ponte Palatino connects Rome's trendy Trastevere section with historic Monte Palatino and the old Roman Forum. The Vestal Virgins were priestesses who lived in the Forum and guarded the Temple of Vesta for 600 years, beginning in the second century B.C. Each year during a summer festival, they would throw straw figurines, or *argei,* into the very river I stood above. This happened during the days of the great Roman Empire, when Vesta, goddess of the hearth, and gods such as Jupiter, Mars, Pluto, and Venus captured much of the empire's imagination and prayers. The Vestals were probably Italy's first group of religious women whose distinctive dress was defined, in part, by a headdress. They wore white *suffibulums,* a type of veil made from squares of linen or undyed cotton. According to some texts, the suffibulums symbolized the women's purity.

The Vestals weren't, however, the first to decorate their hair with fabric. Fashionable Roman women did this all the time, although they preferred to wear streams of thin strips of fabric, similar to ribbons, so as not to cover up their elaborate plaits and curls. Also, women who played sports tied strips of cloth into headbands to hold back their hair. Artistic depictions of these early headpieces are still visible in the ruins of Pompeii and Herculaneum. Nor were Vestals the only women to use the veil as a symbol of commitment. Brides wore veils on their wedding day. Known as *flammeums* because of their "flame-like color," they were shoulder-length, fiery orange cloths

Vestal Virgins were among the first women in the Roman Empire to wear headscarves for religious reasons.

paired with decorative floral head-wreaths. I looked for flammeums while I was in Italy, but most people had no clue what I was talking about. The Vestals, however, were known to just about everyone. Stories still circulate about how the famed virgin priestesses were put to death if they let the eternal flame die out, or—just as earth-shattering—if they had sex.

That was how veils got started in Italy, and they lasted for centuries before everything fell apart. A volcano destroyed Pompeii in A.D. 79; conquests sacked much of the Roman Empire's territory by 150; and Vesta and her mythological family were systematically replaced by Christianity in the late fourth century. From the outset, pagan leaders considered Christianity to be just another cult; they gave it a life span of only 365 years. Proving them wrong, and earning Catholicism the power it has today, are generations of edicts, writings, and rulings. On the topic of women and head coverings, the first official mandate came from the apostle Paul. He wrote, in what is now 1 Corinthians 11:5 in the Bible, that a woman "brings shame on her head if she prays or prophesies bare-headed." Later came Tertullian, the father of Latin Christian writing. (Before Tertullian, Western Christian writing was in Greek.) In 208, while living in Carthage, Tertullian wrote that Christian women should cover their heads before entering a place of worship. Jewish women covered their heads, and Tertullian felt that Christian women should do the same.

The church felt differently. At the beginning of Christendom, when time was still marked with pagan and Jewish chronologies and dates, Christians were persecuted by Diocletian and other pagan leaders for the slightest public display of their new faith. The church was fighting for its survival and would hardly demand that Christians make themselves known. After Constantinople converted to Christianity and the religion was "legalized" within the empire, the church still didn't immediately advocate people dressing in religious garb. This was partly because in some areas, local officials were being elected more for what they wore than for their abilities.

Some women, though, shared Tertullian's view and took it upon themselves to act. They openly defied the empire's laws to publicly embrace Christianity in the most obvious way possible: wearing the veil. Whether they intended their veils to symbolize their spiritual marriage to Christ, as the flammeums did for secular marriages, or their purity and devotion, as the suffibulums did for the Vestals, is not clear. It's not even certain when the wearing of the veil first began or how common it was. What is

Young initiates often wear simple, white head coverings until they are ready for the full habit.

known is that early Christian women remained at home with their parents, wore regular clothes, continued to do their chores, and used the veil to symbolize that they were unavailable to the outside world.

By the fourth century, the church embraced the veil as a sign of religious devotion. Under the *obmubilatio capitis*, or imposition of the veil, it was decreed that the donning of the veil would become the central rite during the consecration of Christian virgins. Pope Liberius was among the first to introduce the veil into a nun's con-

In Rome, nuns from around the world
visit the city's cathedrals.

secration ceremony. According to St. Ambrose, a fourth-century bishop of Milan, his
sister, Marcellina, received a veil from Pope Liberius during her consecration ceremony in St. Peter's Cathedral in Rome around 353.

Among the first church veils were brightly colored flammeums, which rein-
forced the symbolism of the sacred marriage. They eventually gave way to darker,
more somber tones, such as brown and black, in part to represent a woman's death
to the outside world. As convents were built, nuns began to wear uniform clothes—
long robes and collars, mostly. Devoted women gradually became identified by their
total outfit, inadvertently suppressing the primary significance of the veil. Although

the veil was still the essential rite in a consecration ceremony, it was no longer the dominant symbol of a bride of Christ.

The veil's significance diminished even more with the arrival of the Franks, whose own rites of consecration differed from those of the Italians. The Franks, or southern Germans, took control of Italy in 754. Their influence led to completely new rites at the consecration ceremonies, so that by the tenth century, the rite included a crown and a ring. Yet the veil survived, becoming a staple of every nun's religious uniform.

Sister Clare's closet of identical clothes is the modern product of those early days. She is proud of her veil and appreciates the bravery of the first Christian women who risked their lives to wear them.

Before I left Italy, I was invited to a cocktail party at the home of the U.S. ambassador to the Holy See, Corinne "Lindy" Boggs. She lived in a lavish two-story mini-mansion at the top of a secluded, tree-lined drive. There were many priests and nuns present. Feeling self-conscious about my outfit, which was presentable but very simple, I focused on the nuns. They seemed perfectly at home in their clothes, which go from office to evening without so much as a change of shoes. Some of the women's habits were black, others gray. One or two were pastel blue. Some had wide collars, others no collars at all. The veils varied, with subtle differences in length, in the color of the band along the forehead, and in the stiffness of the fabric. Aside from their clothes, the nuns were like all the other guests—rushing for the food, chit-chatting, and having a good time. I decided that if they could be content, even sociable, wearing the same thing every day, then so could I.

The next morning, as if to test my resolve, I spent the day window-shopping. By the time I'd reached the Trevi Fountain and made my way to the Spanish Steps, I couldn't take it anymore. Hundreds of women—none of them nuns—looked fabulous in their up-to-the-minute street fashions, swarming into shops to buy more. I gave up. My brief exercise in modesty turned into a daylong mission to get what I truly wanted. I bought some new clothes.

Images of the Virgin Mary are everywhere in Italy, emphasizing the Christian tradition of modest women wearing head coverings.

France

"There is no woman who does not dream of being dressed in Paris,"
boasted the catalog for the 1925 Paris Exhibition. As much as I loved shopping in Italy, I have to admit that I'm among the wishful dreamers. I made a number of trips to Paris for this project, including one as recently as July 2003, and each time, I explored a different neighborhood, went into dozens of boutiques, and dreamed of owning hundreds of outfits. To my delight, my numerous sojourns took me past incredible window displays of turban-clad mannequins. Whether the mannequins were adorned in chiffon, silk, cotton, or crepe, I imagined their headwraps inspiring passers-by with a new look that has been around for centuries.

Starting in the fifth century, women in France wore headscarves for religious reasons. Thanks to a strong Christian influence, wealthy and poor women wore linen or cotton veils over their hairline and down their shoulders. Some veils were made of transparent silk with colorful embroidery, and many were held in place with thin, flexible bands that wrapped around the forehead.

Developments beyond the veil centered on court life. In the eleventh century, some ladies began wearing a sort of half veil, which covered only the sides of their hair. For this, they used fabric that was cut shorter in the back, leaving an arched opening for their hair to show. A century later, women parted their hair down the middle and wore candy-cane

spiraled ribbons down either side of their hair, sometimes draping it all with a thin scarf or adorning it with a narrow band. Some women also adopted the *barbette*, a two-piece headdress that included a white band that was wrapped over the head and under the chin, and a scarf that was draped on top.

In the fourteenth century, men branched out with stylish *chaperons*, typically flattop turbans made with one end left loose to dangle above the shoulders or fall over one arm. Some were wound vertically; others were wrapped over a *roundlet*, or doughnut-shaped hat. Men had flirted with turbans in the past, but the chaperons were among the most popular styles.

Fashion trends varied little for the next 400 years. Then, in the 1700s, society changed, and with it, so did fashion. Women assumed more public roles, and newly developed public spaces allowed them to be more visible than ever before. Experimental hairstyles and looks, mainly short coiffures with decorative headscarves, became popular. Fabric was important, and a growing number of hairstylists experimented with new textiles and materials. These included the bright madras fabric from India that was popular in the French colonies.

Many new styles came from the royal court at Versailles. Louis XVI's wife, Marie Antoinette, led the way with elaborate headscarves, ribbons, bonnets, and feathers. Her influence lasted until the French Revolution in 1789, when it became instantly

Page 60: Yves Saint Laurent's retirement show on January 22, 2002 featured a retrospective of the designer's controversial 1970 "Forties" collection, in which all the models wore turbans. Page 61 and this page: From the 5th century to the 14th century, headcoverings evolved from simple draped veils to *barbettes* and ribbons that spiraled down long tresses. In the Middle Ages, men throughout western Europe were wearing *chaperons* and other fashionable turbans.

démodé, or unfashionable, to use anything associated with power and prestige. For much of the 1800s, women often twisted gauzy fabrics through their hair. By the 1880s, during France's Belle Epoque, luxury returned with extravagant hats, coiffures, and turbans, some of which were decorated with gold and jewels.

Early in the twentieth century, headwraps took center stage with Paul Poiret's "oriental" line of harem pants and lavish turbans with sprays of feathers. Turbans also appeared as elegant accessories to haute couture, and women experimented with styles that both accented and covered their hair.

While turbans were seen as elegant adornments for the fashionable city dweller, headscarves

Parisian head coverings at the end of the 14th century.

became popular with the country elite. Throughout Europe in the 1920s and 1930s, women took to their cars, boats, and country homes while wearing silk *foulards*, or large scarves, that were folded into triangles with the ends tied under the chin. Smaller some scarves were turned into headbands and ponytail holders for the new generation of athletic women.

Quite unexpectedly, turbans took over with force in the 1940s. World War II had started, and wartime restrictions challenged women into embracing new fashions. "From 1942 to '46, it was a difficult time," remembered François Lesage, a second-generation French embroiderer whose family business has been a part of haute couture

Turbans, which were an occasional fashion accessory in the early 1900s, became a daily necessity during World War II.

since 1924. "We had to have tickets to get everything—soap, bread, chocolate, oil, everything. Things were hard to come by, including shampoo. [Women] couldn't wash their hair as often as they wanted, so they wore turbans." Turbans were also practical for women who took to the assembly lines to replace the male workforce that had gone off to fight in the war.

Finding interesting textiles from which to make attractive turbans was a challenge. "Silk was almost nowhere to be found, and tickets for buying fabric lasted until 1950," said Lesage. As a result, cotton and soft, jersey fabrics became increasingly popular. Ads for René Véron, Madame Grés, Evelyne Arzan, and others showed how these fabrics could be folded and twisted into a variety of elegant turbans. There was no shame in wearing turbans, and many prominent women did so. The author Simone de Beauvoir and Madame Grés, the couturiere who designed Greek-inspired draped gowns, both wore turbans. In fact, Madame Grés later admitted to *Women's Wear Daily* that she only began wearing turbans in the early 1940s when she couldn't get to a salon and she wanted to hide her hair.

Turbans were still occasionally worn in the 1950s, but most women went back

Hermès's signature equestrian-decorated scarves first appeared in 1937, just as women were adopting more sporty fashions. This is an advertisement from the 1960s for Hermès's "Belle-île: le port" scarf.

Lanvin's black silk tiara headscarf, designed by Elber Albaz.

to headscarves. "The fashion was called a *bandeau*," said Lesage. "Women in Paris were riding bikes and mopeds and driving around in convertibles. The bandeau gave them a sense of freedom, and all the women wore it." The bandeau was a long satiny-silk scarf folded into a narrow strip and worn like a headband. The ends were tied at the nape of the neck and left to hang down the back.

Headwraps and headscarves remained on the periphery until 1971, when the esteemed fashion designer Yves Saint Laurent did the unthinkable. He presented his "Forties" collection, which featured a fabulous array of turbans. Most were deep, vertical wraps with loose folds and bright colors. Some had creative touches, such as a small fan above the forehead made from pleating one of the ends of the fabric. Not since World War II had turbans been presented as a significant part of fashion. The show revived memories of the war and occupation and reopened scars that were barely healed. For that, Saint Laurent received harsh criticism. One magazine called the show "a tour de force of bad taste."

Still, turbans had become an undeniable presence in fashion, and within a few years, they were back on Parisian runways. Among those leading the pack in the 1980s was the Japanese-born designer Kenzo Takada, who was frequently inspired by ethnic looks. From the 1990s through today, designs from Karl Lagerfeld at Chanel, Alber Elbaz, Christian Lacroix, and Jean Paul Gaultier, among others, have been presented at one time or another with turbans or headscarves.

"Turbans do a wonderful job of framing the face," said Jean Paul Gaultier in an e-mail interview after his spring 2000 couture show. In that show, most of his models wore turbans made from soft fabrics wrapped in a single layer around the base of the head, then formed into a vertical roll of folds and tucks. Those that didn't wear fabric turbans had hairstyles that were done up to resemble turbans. "I was inspired during a recent trip to India, where everyone wore turbans, even the pilot," Gaultier said.

Suzy Menkes, the fashion and style editor for the *International Herald Tribune*, commenting on Gaultier's show, said, "Turbans make wonderful accessories, and I'm always interested in how Jean Paul Gaultier carries out his ideas. Although he is a Western designer, he seems very interested in ethnic elements. The turbans that year were another example of how he cares about the total look."

Over lunch in a brasserie along Boulevard Charles de Gaulle, Menkes and I talked about a number of designers and the role headwraps and headscarves have played in their collections. The conversation led to Alber Elbaz and the House of Lanvin's sumptuously soft, black silk headscarves with decorative tiaras made from carefully placed antique crystals. The scarves are two and a half feet square, and the tiaras range from four and a half to six inches wide. They first appeared in October 2002 with Lanvin's summer 2003 collection and sold out within months of appearing in stores. "I think it was a very original and brilliant idea," said Menkes. "Crowns and tiaras are very much in style. Elbaz did it as a sort of fashion fusion, bringing together two popular elements of fashion."

"Headwraps are beautiful accessories to a woman's wardrobe. I don't see them ever going out of style," she added.

Russia

After Paris, my journey took me to Moscow, St. Petersburg, and the rural towns in between. Within days of landing at Moscow's drab, Communist-era airport, my translator secured an unexpected interview for me with a Chechen woman named Zolpa. To reach her, I had to take a forty-minute cab ride from the center of Moscow to a dilapidated apartment complex in a seedy part of town. It was so far off the tourist trail that no amount of money in my budget would convince the driver to wait.

Zolpa's apartment was on the fifth floor of the third tower from the street—a sparsely furnished one-bedroom that she shared with her ten-year-old daughter and her sixty-eight-year-old father. Zolpa herself was about thirty. Her daughter knew one English word, and she absolutely glowed when she got her chance to use it for the first time. She said "Hello" maybe three times before she politely exchanged my sneakers for a pair of house slippers, then played for most of the evening with Barbie dolls and a McDonald's Happy Meal toy. We all sat in the TV room as Zolpa and her father told me about the role headwraps and other headdresses play in Chechnya, and how different things were now that they lived in Moscow.

"A Chechen woman's scarf has a very symbolic meaning," Zolpa began, speaking softly and quickly to my guide, Dasha, who then translated her words to me. "It has the power to stop a fight when nothing else can, and was once even used to help end a war." Chechen women, like their mothers and grandmothers, start wearing scarves around the age of fifteen, the same age that boys frequently begin to "take up arms," she said, referring to the common practice of teenage boys carrying guns to help fight for Chechnya's independence. Scarves are always worn outside of the home, and sometimes inside, especially when older people come to visit. "I was taught that women should be modest and respectful, and that when God looks down on women, he's never supposed to see their hair," Zolpa said. The exact moment a girl starts wearing a scarf varies, and some resist it because it spells the end of their childhood. Zolpa, however, said she started wearing a scarf without ever being told to do so. "Once, on a tram, I saw an old man spit on a girl about the same age as me who didn't have her head covered. I hid myself in the crowd and went home. Before I went out again, I put on a scarf," she recalled.

Headscarves were such a serious matter that if a woman ever took hers off in public, it was a signal that something was very wrong. "That's how she could stop a fight," Zolpa explained. "If a woman takes off her scarf and throws it between two men that are fighting, the men stop. They have to. It's that serious."

Zolpa's father, going back and forth between the Chechen and Russian languages, told the story of a "very tall and beautiful Chechen woman" who, wearing a

Page 68: Traditional dress in pre-Czarist Russia. Page 69, left: In the early years of Czarist Russia, lavish new fashions were combined with traditional costumes; right: A girl in rural Russian dress. This page: Regional headdresses worn by a merchant's wife from Kalouga (left), a Karbardinian woman (center) and a Votlakin woman (right).

A Tartar national dance performed in the Caucusus mountains. All heads are covered.

long, white headscarf, had placed herself in front of soldiers and tanks as a white flag of surrender to the Tartar-Mongols in the fourteenth century. "She was very brave," he said.

Zolpa explained that scarves also serve as a visible sign of a girl's maturity and her willingness to get married. In a family with more than one daughter, the eldest puts the scarf on first. She hopefully gets married quickly, then the second eldest puts hers on. "But if the second one is an adult and the first one still hasn't married, then she puts it on anyway because God should not see her hair, and also, she has no chance of finding a husband if her head isn't covered."

After a couple of hours in the sitting room, we moved around the corner to the kitchen, where we sat at a small, aluminum table and Zolpa began preparing steamed dumplings from an old Kazakhstan recipe. Zolpa spoke about the difficulty of adjusting to life in Moscow. She said that she wore her scarf for five or six years after she moved to Moscow, but then had to stop. "People in Moscow knew I was from Chech-

Two Tartar women wear headscarves on their way to work in the fields.

nya or another republic because of my scarf. I couldn't get a job, and I was getting stopped by the police all the time," she said. She and other immigrants had many discussions about whether women should still wear scarves—in Moscow and in Chechnya. "The first time I left the house without my scarf in Moscow, I felt naked, but then I talked to other immigrants who'd moved to Moscow, and we all agreed it was for the best. Unfortunately, back home those who don't wear scarves are considered immoral, and men think that women taking off their scarves is just the beginning of worse things to come."

Zolpa's part of town is home to thousands of immigrants from former republics of the old Soviet Union. Like Zolpa, many of them have abandoned their traditional clothes, including their headdresses. Young Ukrainian girls no longer tie yellow, blue, pink, and gold ribbons in their hair. Uzbeki men no longer wear turbans (embroidered cloth wrapped around the bottom of a hat, or *tyubeteika,* for young married men, and round turbans made from strips of white cloth for older men). Rural Uzbek women now living in Moscow rarely throw a shawl, or *khalat,* over their heads and shoulders when they go out, and the wealthier ones don't often cover their heads with longer khalats called *paranjas.* Caucasian and Trans-Caucasian girls don't wear their simple headscarves tied in a knot in the back anymore, a ritual young girls from the region once observed every day until they were married. And the married women no longer drape silk scarves on top of embroidered, brimless caps, securing the ends loosely around their necks as their ancestors did. Some traditional women may still wear dark scarves after they've given birth to their first child, but not many.

This almost complete abandonment of traditional dress didn't happen only among immigrants from the outer republics. Russia has had its fair share of costume changes and over the centuries has also walked away from traditional headscarves and other head coverings.

Up until the tenth century, clothes in Russia were as distinctive as they were varied. Women dressed according to the style of their village, region, and socioeconomic class. They wore richly embroidered clothes such as *ponyovas* (long, flared skirts) and *navershniks* (loose-fitting tops). It was a pagan society, and women placed a great deal of pride and superstition in how they covered their hair. They believed it was dangerous for the sun to touch their hair and that great harm would come to their families and livestock if it did. Only unmarried girls went out bareheaded, keeping their hair in one long braid. Long hair was a sign that they were healthy and would make good wives. Once they reached puberty, girls tied red ribbons at the ends of their braids to signify they'd matured to childbearing age and were officially ready to be married.

Traditional bridal headdress on display in the State Russian Museum.

Married women wore a variety of elaborate headdresses, which could consist of twenty different parts each and weigh up to eleven pounds. In some regions, a newlywed's first headdress was a *babya kika*, a combination of a wreath and a headwrap made with a thin, brightly colored scarf called an *urbus*. In most regions, after a woman had her second or third healthy child she switched to wearing headscarves, which were usually two- to two-and-a-half-foot squares of crimson red or jet black fabric with bold floral patterns and fringes along the edges. The colors of the scarves were often connected to the soil. In parts of the country with black dirt, the ponyovas and scarves were black or dark blue. In areas with brown or red-clay dirt, the ponyovas and scarves were red. Head- dresses were the most attractive and expensive part of a woman's ensemble, even among peasant women. They were routinely made with velvet, damask, and silk and ornamented with pearls and precious stones.

In the tenth century, when Christianity began to penetrate Russia, the Orthodox Church brought

An 1880 painting of a Russian mother holding her child. She wears a fur cap over her headscarf.

sweeping changes to the lifestyle and status of Russian women. Whereas before, women were often considered equal to men, they were now told to be subservient to their husbands. The babya kika and other headwraps were redefined. Scarves continued to be worn outside but were now worn out of modesty and respect for God, and women were compelled to keep them on when entering a place of worship.

The end of traditional dress began in 1700. Peter the Great, czar of Russia, saw traditional dress as backward. He wanted his people to dress like the French and enforced that desire with a series of executive orders called *ukases,* which outlawed traditional clothes and outlined the Western-style fashions to be worn instead. In the villages, word often came later, and rural fashions were routinely out of date. Initially, Russians protested Peter's ukases, but toward the end of his rule the new costumes had become widely popular.

The ukases didn't immediately mean the end of headscarves and other headdresses, but people were hard-pressed to find creative ways to integrate old traditions with new fashions. One of the most successful compromises came from loosely wrapping a scarf, or *fata*, around a traditional Russian hat, the *kokoshnik*. *Kokosh* means "sitting hen," and the kokoshnik, a close-fitting, bulbous hat with a high front, had been worn by women in the central and northern territories of Russia for centuries. With the fata wrapped around it, the newly styled kokoshnik resembled the onion domes on top of Russia's Orthodox churches. It became one of the most popular accessories of the eighteenth century.

Headscarves remained indispensable for at least another century, but the traditional ways of wearing them finally fell out of favor as women grew more active in sports, developed their own social lives, and became more aware of modern fashions from the West. The Great October Revolution of 1917, which saw the downfall of czarist Russia and the rise of communism, also radically changed Russian life, affecting popular culture and dress. The working class came to power, allowing women to take jobs and become more visible. As in France, the new female workforce quickly saw headscarves as a useful tool to contain their long hair.

Today, traditional dress has no place in Moscow or St. Petersburg, except in the permanent collections at The Hermitage and in the ethnic wing of the State Russian Museum. Also, the Russian National Library has a wonderful collection of out-of-print books that record the history of costumes. But like Zolpa's daughter, who is growing up in a world without traditional garb, Russian children are largely unaware of headscarves. For them, there are wonderful theme restaurants where waitresses dressed in the traditional costumes of former republics bring out heaping portions of each region's cuisine. The food is not always as good as Zolpa's dumplings, and the history may not be as personal as her stories, but it's a start.

A promotional poster depicting the Soviet working woman, wearing her headscarf.

The Czech Republic

The worst stuff happens when I'm feeling my best. Did I mention before that my entire budget for the Sahel was stolen at the airport in Abidjan, Côte d'Ivoire? Or that I left my camera and passport in a Metro station in Paris? On both occasions, my spirits were high and things had been going really well with the trip. Yet, as bad as those setbacks were, they were nothing compared to the tragedy awaiting me in Prague. Just as I started to unpack, I discovered that my entire canister of Ghirardelli hot cocoa mix had emptied out into my luggage. It was a present from a woman in Russia, whose friends had shipped it to her from San Francisco. Ignoring the heartbreaking loss of prize comfort food for a moment, consider the material damage: Everything in my bag—and later the hotel room—was dusted with brown powder. To make matters worse, a tube of moisturizer had burst, adding clumps of chocolate goo to the already massive cleanup.

Breathe.

Crisis aside, I only had five days to seek out *kroje*, the Czech Republic's distinctive national costumes. Turning a blind eye to the beautiful crystal, handmade lace, and nightly puppet theaters that make Prague so interesting, I left the center of Bohemia and traveled south to the land of Moravia. As far back as the ninth century, the Bohemians and Moravians both developed village-specific kroje. In the mid-1800s, Bohemians began abandoning kroje for Western European dress; the Moravians adopted some aspects of Western dress (as well as elements of Turkish and Far Eastern

Previous spread (left to right): 1920 portrait of woman from Moravia, wearing the popular red, Turkish-influenced scarf; 1916 oil painting of a peasant girl from Veselany, Moravia by Joza Uprka; woman from Detva, Slovakia painted by Vladimir Droppa.

dress) but steadfastly held on to their own traditions. It was those traditions I'd come to investigate.

I spent most of my time in Strážnice, a small town with two hotels, three churches, a music school, a castle, and a national folk institute. The town dates back to the thirteenth century and was once the biggest in southeast Moravia. After its peak of prosperity in the seventeenth century, the Industrial Age passed it by and the town declined. Then, in the early 1900s, Strážnice reinvented itself as a center for arts, education, and folk culture.

Today, everyone in Strážnice wears jeans, T-shirts, and other modern clothes, as people do throughout Moravia. But stored neatly in trunks at home are their traditional kroje, which they wear during local celebrations and pass down as heirlooms. There are as many as 550 kroje styles in the Czech Republic, each of which includes a unique headdress that identifies a person's village, marital status, the event he or she is attending, and the role he or she will be playing at the event.

The two oil paintings by Jóža Uprka on this spread depict village women from Vicnov (opposite page) and Kunovice (this page), wearing traditional Moravian headscarves.

Men wear hats and women wear headscarves, bonnets, caps, or a creative combination of all three. Some traditional headscarves are incredibly complicated. Like nautical knots, they are tied in a precise fashion, whether wound around the head and tucked under, gathered into wide pleats at the ears with triangular folds jutting from underneath, or looped around bonnets with the ends hanging loosely past the knees.

The *satka,* a long strip of woven material, was the original women's headscarf. It was often wrapped around a cap and was usually embroidered, decorated with dried fish scales, or both. The Turks later introduced a large, cranberry red scarf with floral designs that was quickly incorporated into new kroj styles throughout Moravia. A piece of cardboard was often sewn onto the inside of the fabric to keep the headscarf stiff.

Headdresses were considered an essential part of a woman's complete outfit. They were popularized around the 1400s, when villages were isolated from each other and developed their own individual styles. Marriages between men and women from different villages were rare, but every so often, a rich woman from a

A woman from the Balta region of southern Bohemia wears a large, elaborately beaded headscarf called a *plena*.

small town might marry a poor man from a big city. Such a match would increase her social standing, and she would move to the city to be with her husband. When this happened, she had to abandon the kroj of her village for the costumes and customs of her new home.

The transition from kroje to modern dress was gradual. In the 1800s, Bohemian and Moravian peoples began wearing Western clothes, which they found easier to work in and maintain. At the same time, a wave of pan-Slovak nationalists promoted efforts to increase the region's spirit of nationalism. The Slovak poet Ján Kollár wrote in the early 1800s that "life consists not only of bread, money, profit and benefit but also of beauty, joy, gratitude to our forefathers and loving respect for traditional dress and folklore." Folk festivals were organized, the first of which was the Ethnographic Czech-Slovonic Exhibition in Prague in 1895. Along with traditional dress, it featured handicrafts from different Czech and Slovak regions.

Kroje were banned in 1939 by the Nazis, then again under Communist rule after World War II. At both times, kroje were considered nationalistic, and anyone wearing a kroj was judged to be a dissident. Many kroje were confiscated, prompting families to smuggle their heirlooms out of the country. With each liberation, Moravians and Bohemians gathered in the streets in their traditional costumes. Still, children and working women had less of an interest in making and wearing kroje like their parents. In 1946, to prevent the obsolescence of kroje, Strážnice and the International Folk Institute created the International Folkloric Festival, which has grown into the Czech Republic's largest event of this type. Villagers throughout Moravia and Bohemia, as well as people from neighboring Slovakia, Hungary, Austria, and other countries, come to celebrate traditional customs and dress.

In the summer, when the festival occurs, yellow canola flowers blanket the countryside and the picturesque town of Strážnice, with its A-frame, red-shingled

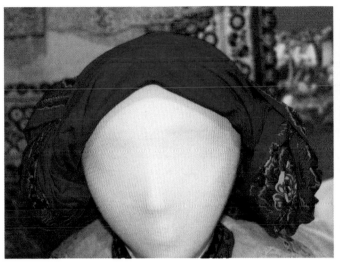

houses and vast meadows, becomes as popular a destination as Prague. "We look forward to it every year," said a teacher in southwest Moravia. She added, "My daughter joined the dance troupe two years ago and wears my old kroje. I'm so proud of her. I used to dance in the festivals myself, when I was younger. Now I look after the clothes and make sure everyone is dressed properly. Most people can't tie their own headscarves, so I do it for them. I try to teach them, but they always forget by the next summer."

Above and left: In Moravia, scarves can be draped, knotted, and tied to produce various styles. They are an integral part of the kroje.

Turkey

In Istanbul, public transportation is to taxis what peanut butter and jelly sandwiches are to filet mignon. Nothing fancy, but sometimes exactly what you need. Lucky for me, I like PB&J, and I liked taking the bus in Turkey. Of course, I didn't always get a seat, and half the time I couldn't pronounce where I was going, but the drivers were helpful and it was a rush to find the right bus going in the right direction, and then hop off at a new stop in some as-yet-to-be-discovered part of the city. I stayed in the Sultanahmet district in a modest hotel within walking distance of the Topkapi Palace Museum. For one week, I lived on fresh cherries and hot *lachman-jem*, a poor man's meal akin to thin-crust pizza. My itinerary started at Topkapi Palace, which I believed would be a font of information on turbans in the Ottoman era. I was wrong. Had I been traveling the world to research porcelain dishes, handkerchiefs, or iron helmets, then the palace would have been perfect. Disappointed, I turned to touring the city by bus on $2 a day, scavenging for information on my own.

The Turks speak rarely of turbans these days, but up until 1839 they were the pride of the Ottoman Empire. Every man—Muslim and non-Muslim—wore one—with the exception of a few military officers, who wore some of those iron helmets on display in the palace.

It is believed that the word "turban" has one of two possible origins: It could have come from the Persian word for

Page 82: During the Ottoman Empire, Turkish women often covered their heads with two-piece muslin veils called *mahrems*. Page 83: Various turban styles from the Ottoman Empire (left) and an Armenian merchant during the same period (right).
This page, above: 16th century miniature of a sultan and his advisors.
Right: Ottoman coin depicting Sultan Muhammet the Conqueror.

tulips *(türblents)*, which grew wild across the Asiatic steppe, or from the Turkish word for a headpiece or scarf *(tulbend)*, which in turn was also used to denote tulips. Turbans were initially worn to protect men from severe temperatures. Then, in the 1200s, when Islam came to the region, turbans became a necessary component of prayer. It was believed that a man's prayer was more valued by Allah if he wore a turban. Turbans carried so much meaning that men removed them when using the bathroom. The only other place turbans were not worn as a general rule was inside the palace walls. There, they were the privileged accoutrements of only the most powerful men.

The founder of the Ottoman Empire and first sultan, Osman I, wore a small white turban wrapped around a three- or four-inch-high dome-shaped cap. One end of the turban hung over the side of his temple. The style was native to Khorasan, a region near the Anatolian Mountains, and worn by every sultan until the late 1400s, when Sultan Mehmed II acceded to the throne. Known as Mehmed the Conqueror, he changed everything about Ottoman headdresses. He created a system of hierarchies that distinguished a person's status by the color, size, material, and design of his clothing. Peasants were not allowed to wear yellow boots or slippers; the elaborate costumes of water carriers had to be made of inexpensive cloth; and Jews, Christians, and other non-Muslims were forbidden to wear green turbans.

The turbans Mehmed II created, some based on regional styles, were wrapped over skullcaps or tall, cylindrical hats, with the hat visible or not, depending on the style. Within the government, more than a hundred different types of

headgear were used to designate rank and office. The largest and most stylish turbans were worn by senior judges, military justices, doctors, and magistrates. From then on, the sultan's turban was usually decorated with an egret's plume and a jeweled brooch. If the sultan was short, or pudgy, he often wore a taller, more imposing turban. The first sultans, like most men, wrapped their own turbans. Occasionally, if the turban was particularly well-wound and intricate, it would be carefully removed at night and placed on

Top to bottom: The style native to Khorsan, worn by Sultan Osman, the Ottoman Empire's founding sultan; Turban of the "ship's captain," worn by the Second Captain of the Navy; Headgear of the "Sergeant of the Chamber" in the Ottoman Empire's Maritime arsenal; Turban worn by Sultan Mehmed IV.

a shelf to be reworn the next morning. As the empire grew, the office of turban bearer, or *telbentar agha,* was created. This courtier was solely responsible for creating and maintaining the sultan's headpieces and always had two spare turbans wrapped, pinned together, and ready to wear.

For awhile, the exotic costumes were like banners advertising the Ottomans' military might. For 500 years, the Ottomans conquered foreign lands, so that at the peak of their power, they ruled as far north as Hungary and as far south as the Barbary Coast of North Africa. By the late 1700s, the Ottomans had begun losing more battles than they were winning, and their costumes became the focus of anecdotes in tales of military defeat. In his book *The Ottoman Centuries* (1977), Lord Kinross, describing the 1799 Ottoman defeat against Napoleon in Aboukir, Greece, wrote that Napoleon drove the Turks into the sea, "where the waters of the bay bobbed with their turbans as they drowned by the thousand."

Selim III, sultan from 1789 to 1807, declared that turbans and other traditional customs were signs of the Ottomans' medieval backwardness. Hoping to reinvigorate the empire, he brought in European advisers to train and re-dress his troops. Almost immediately, his soldiers revolted, and within days, Selim III was put to death.

Where Selim III failed, his cousin, Sultan Mahmud II, succeeded. With a calculated plan that included sharing his ideas with the *ulema,* or religious overseers, Mahmud II initiated a series of sumptuary laws in 1829 that effectively abolished the turban. Its place was taken by the fez, which at the time was seen as very modern and European. Forcing men to give up their turbans wasn't easy. The head was considered sacred, and how one covered it was important. The turban had become a symbol of religious devotion. To replace it with Western fashion was a radical act. Riots broke out, but Mahmud II prevailed. Men finally came around and embraced the fez.

The new look lasted until November 25, 1925, when the president of the newly created Republic of Turkey enacted the Hat Law, replacing the fez with the bowler. Mustafa Kemal, later known as Atatürk, or the father of Turkey, was the country's first president. In 1922, he reportedly said that within two years, every man would "wear a hat instead of a fez and every woman have her face uncovered."

Traditionally, women never left the home without their headscarves and cloaks. The problem with Atatürk's reforms was that a lot of women liked tradition. Turkish women's head coverings have as much of a colorful and legendary history as those of

Before the reforms of 1925, most women kept themselves covered in veils and headscarves.

the men's. Through the centuries, women had developed elegant styles that made ample use of a variety of colors and fabrics. The scarves didn't always provide full coverage; in the Middle Ages, many scarves were loosely wound to reveal locks of hair. Outside of Istanbul, brides from Kozak and other regions wore layers of bright red and blue headscarves and small turbans, often decorated with strings of silver coins and various jewels.

Women in Istanbul in the early 1900s, before Atatürk passed his dress code reforms.

The reforms in 1925 sought to liberate women from their Islamic-based veils and head-scarves, which by then had become more muted and somber than those worn in the fourteenth century. In 1981, headscarves were banned in public schools, and in 1998, in all government institutions. By then, 99 percent of Turkey's population was Muslim. The reforms were not aimed at regional and fashion-oriented head coverings. Many Muslims however, felt that covering their heads was an important tradition to continue, and Islamic traditionalists protested the changes.

Not all headscarves were considered religious. A fashionably wrapped scarf, or one that was simply worn to protect a woman from the weather, was completely ac-ceptable in the new secular state. But the basortü, a style of head tie closely resem-bling the hijab, was seen as an Islamic statement. Women who wore the basortü were labeled as Islamic traditionalists. In 1982, in protest of the first ban on religious headscarves, students wearing basortüs refused to remove them in class and were suspended or expelled. After that, there were dozens of instances of women being reprimanded, expelled from school, or fired from their jobs for not removing their head coverings.

I traveled to Ankara, the capital, to speak to Merve Kavakci, one of the country's most vocal opponents of the ban on scarves. Kavakci was elected to a seat in Parliament in 1999 but was kept from taking her oath because she refused to remove her headscarf. She invited me to her home, where we spoke while her children were in school. "This is similar to the civil rights struggle of black Americans in the '60s," she said in perfect English. (Kavakci lived in the United States for ten years and went to college in Texas before returning to Turkey to enter politics.) She said she had campaigned in her basortü and that her constituents expected her to always wear it. "I am not a dissident and I don't want to make trouble. This is a complex issue of politics, religion, democracy, and human rights. I am Muslim, and I should be allowed to cover my head whenever and however I want."

Many women, however, liked Atatürk's reforms, which also gave women the right to vote and own property. An architect in Istanbul said she would never have been able to start her own business, or show authority over her contractors, without the reforms. "My mother and grandmothers covered every day. They could never go outside and feel the air, or go on a boat and feel the mist. My mother still covers. I hate it, and I would never want to live like that," she said.

My short stay and brief interviews barely skimmed the surface of the complexities of Turkish headwear, but the journey proved to be a valuable introduction that would later help me in the Middle East and in Asia.

Middle East / West Asia

No 616.

Israel

I arrived in Israel with my fair share of misconceptions. I thought that I would land in a war zone. Violent episodes—suicide bombings and military incursions—had been reported in the weeks before my trip, and I had no reason to expect they would stop. I also believed there'd be a wall of security at the airport, and so I'd left my knife in a storage unit in Paris. My little steel companion, called "The Traveler" by the Chicago company that makes it, is a razor-sharp, six-inch, flip-out blade, and it had been with me since my journey began. I hated to leave it behind, but I figured it was the best thing to do. As it turned out, I arrived in Tel Aviv without incident. With no visible signs of war, the city was beautiful and unexpectedly calm.

My initial walk about town revealed yet another misconception I'd had. I had expected to see ultra-Orthodox Jews in traditional dress. Instead, while strolling past bagel shops, lingerie boutiques, tattoo parlors, and fast-food restaurants, I saw a lot of women in animal-print tops and spandex pants. More important, the only thing many women in Tel Aviv (and Jerusalem and Nazareth) used to cover their hair was hairspray. A Jewish scholar told me later that I should have known that any part of town with tattoo parlors wouldn't be frequented by Hasidic Jews. I later learned that there are many Orthodox women in Israel who wear headscarves, wigs of varying degrees of quality, hats and snoods (large stockings of loose material), depending on their sect. Head coverings and clothes are usually black for men, while women's headscarves tend to be more colorful.

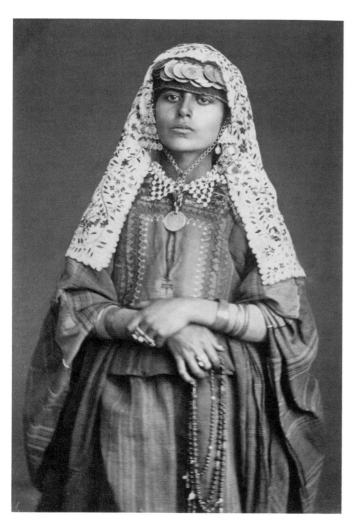

Page 92: A Bedouin wears a heavy *agal* to hold his *kuffiya* in place. Page 93: Girls and young women were not obliged to cover their entire heads, but were generally expected to wear head coverings when venturing outside. This page: Bedouin girls often adorned their head coverings with heavy silver coins.

Much of what is known about early Middle Eastern dress—including floppy hats, turbans, and scarves—comes from monuments, marble reliefs, and written documents that date back to biblical times. One of the earliest recorded headpieces was an *agal*, a goat's-hair cord used interchangeably as a headband and a camel hobble. Later, in a style borrowed from the Bedouins, a neighboring nomadic people, ancient Hebrews folded a square cloth, called a *kaffiyah*, into a triangle to form a headscarf. Two corners were knotted together under their chins, and the other one hung down in the back to protect the nape of the neck against the sun. On top of that, they continued to use the agal, which kept the kaffiyah firmly in place.

A variety of hats and headwrap styles were later introduced by foreigners, including the Assyrians and the Babylonians in biblical times, the Turks, Greeks, and Romans through the sixteenth century, and others well into modern times. Fringed, unbleached cotton, black cashmere, white muslin, or yellow and red striped kaffiyahs were worn over the centuries, sometimes with an agal, other times wound loosely on the head or over caps. Books on early Israeli dress have noted that turbans routinely morphed into portable pillows and also provided storage for important papers.

Stories from the Bible are frequently used as examples of early Hebrew dress by rabbis and scholars, including many of the people I interviewed in Israel and New York. In the Bible, turbans were included in a list of clothes for Moses to give to his brother Aaron in order to give him "dignity and magnificence" (Exodus 28:2–4). From biblical times into the first centuries of the common era, Jewish priests wore mitres—sometimes bulbous hats, other times turbans made from thick swaths of wool or linen, sometimes embroidered. Turbans were often stitched into a cap and covered with another piece of linen.

Pinpointing exactly when headscarves began to have a religious significance is a near impossible task for even the best scholars and archeologists, who frequently

Left: Arab men wearing *kuffiyas* in three different styles.
Below: A Bedoin dressed for the desert.

challenge the dates and findings of their predecessors as new information continues to be compiled. It is, however, generally agreed that, as early as the first century, the colors and fabrics people wore were increasingly governed by laws based on the teachings of the Scriptures and the Talmud. In different regions, and at different times over the course of many centuries in the Jewish diaspora, clothes could not be made from pigskin, and they had to be removed in a certain order before taking a bath. Mourners, and those accused of adultery, were expected to wear black, a color otherwise not typically worn among early Hebrews. White was worn at weddings and other festivals. Women were not to wear red because it was regarded as licentious, and purple was the color of royalty, with sumptuary laws forbidding it to be worn by commoners.

A young Bedouin girl in full headdress.

As for the veils, "one reference we have is that when Rebecca sees Isaac, she veils herself," said Dr. Yaakov Elman, associate professor of Judaic Studies at Yeshiva University in New York and currently a Harry Starr Fellow at Harvard University, referring to Genesis 24:65, which he said could reflect Mesopotamian mores of the early or mid–second millennium.

A series of laws about head coverings existed for married women. Being bareheaded was labeled "an indecorous form of 'ervah," or nakedness, for married women and was blamed for causing improper glances from men. Married women were forbidden to let any of their hair show and obligated to secure their scarves accordingly. If a married woman's hair was uncovered, it became unlawful to recite the Shema, the Jewish holy prayer, in her presence. Married women never went outside or received guests in their home without covering their heads, and the more pious women covered their hair even in the privacy of their homes. In Babylonian Talmud, Yoma 47A, there is a story of a woman who predicted that her sons would become priests. When asked why, she said it was because not even the beams of her house had ever seen her hair. "In the last few centuries in Central Europe, some women even shaved off their hair before putting on a scarf," explained Dr. Elman, referring to a custom that is still followed among some Orthodox groups. A hefty fine was imposed on any man that removed a woman's headscarf in the street, and according to the Mishna, the code of Jewish law dating back to 220 C.E., a man was given grounds for divorce if his wife went outside with her head uncovered (Mishna Ketubot 7:6). "This is a very sensitive issue," explained Dr. Elman. "Among some right-wing Orthodox circles, it arouses a passion like nobody's business. Even today, a person can insult his opponent by saying something like 'Your mother went out with her hair uncovered.'"

As early as 100 B.C.E., women wore khalaks—headscarves that reached their knees. For weddings, grooms wore small turbans called pe'ers, and brides wore veils. The most common type of bridal veil was a one-piece scarf that simply draped over the bride's face. Less common was a two-piece covering, including a top cloth that fell above the bride's eyes, and a second one that was fixed over the bridge of her nose and hung down over her chest. Bridal veils are also mentioned in the Bible, particularly in Genesis 29, when Jacob, believing he was marrying Rachel, married Leah instead. The Bible doesn't describe the type of veil Leah wore. For this, we are at the mercy of archeological evidence, according to many scholars, who insist there is no way to know exactly what was worn, why, or how.

Women's head coverings among Jews living in Palestine varied little until the 1800s, when waves of European Jews began to resettle the region, introducing new clothing and headdress styles. Turbans, which ranged from round and bulbous to oval and almost elliptical, became popular. They were often decorated with gold chains, pearls, jewels, and long trains of diaphanous or embroidered fabric. Not only worn by men, turbans were fashionable among married women and many young girls as well. Traditionalists didn't care for the new look and pressed for maintaining the old ways. Ultra-Orthodox Jews banded together, establishing their own neigh-

Nineteenth century illustration of Jewish family on Mt. Zion.

borhoods, schools, and synagogues. Men adopted black bowlers instead of keeping the kaffiyahs and turbans, but ultra-Orthodox women continued to wear head-scarves.

Although the kaffiyah—more commonly pronounced *kuffiya* among Arabs—was abandoned by Jews in the early 1900s, it was increasingly embraced by Palestinians. Kuffiyas, once associated with rural laborers, had long been worn by Arab men to keep their hair out of their faces and to protect them from the sun. As Islam spread in the seventh century, head cloths became a part of Muslim dress. Today, Palestinians and other Arabs throughout the Middle East and the Arabian (Persian) Gulf region continue to wear kuffiyas and other head coverings, generally referred to as *hattas*, as a tribute to their heritage.

By the early 1900s, the British had gained a hold on Palestine. They brought with them new fashions, foods, and customs that penetrated Palestinian life. In 1936, an anti-British rebellion erupted pitting the Arabs of Palestine against Britons and Jews. During the fighting, Arab soldiers wore hattas as a de facto symbol of their resistance and their struggle for independence.

The fighting, of course, continues. Today, access to the Occupied Territories is frequently limited to official personnel during heightened periods of violence. My trip coincided with one such period, and I was not allowed to enter predominantly Palestinian districts. Fortunately, a number of Palestinians living in other parts of Israel and abroad were willing to share their traditions with me.

Palestinian kuffiyas are generally black and white checked. Head coverings in other Arab countries may be red and white checked, brown and white checked, solid white, or white with red, black, or brown stripes along the edge.

Yasser Arafat, the leader of the Palestinian Liberation Organization, is probably the most universally recognized Palestinian. What's not widely known is that the shape of his signature black and white kuffiya is carefully fashioned to represent a map of Palestine—and its meaning has thus been the subject of controversy. The kuffiya has become his trademark. According to his aides and people close to him, Arafat uses the kuffiya to pay tribute to his native culture and tradition and as a symbol of the continued Palestinian struggle for independence.

As a young man in the 1940s and early 1950s, Arafat, like most young men, wore head coverings sporadically, usually only when working outside. Because head coverings were associated with the fighters for independence, they were generally reserved for adults and older boys. But in 1956, Arafat traveled to Prague to attend a meeting of the International Students' Congress. It was his first trip abroad, and for the first time, he wore a head covering as a symbol of his heritage. He wore a hatta

In the 1800s, waves of European Jews settled in the region. They introduced new fashions, including this Ottoman-style headdress.

and an agal. From then on, he was rarely seen without a head covering.

Today, hattas are not as popular among Palestinians as they once were, particularly among young men and business professionals who have to work in Israel. Even so, they have not disappeared and can be seen during any Palestinian celebration. A Palestinian woman's traditional headscarf, called a *tarha*, is a large cloth that covers her head and falls to her waist. It was worn as early as the fifth century, often over small caps, turbans, or smaller headscarves. Islam in the seventh century prompted many Arab women to wear hijabs and large scarves, generally alone or under tarhas, which cover a woman's hairline as a sign of her modesty.

Tarhas were originally handwoven with lavish embroidery that illustrated a woman's skill, personality, and the style of her particular village. The patterns included symbols of hope, prosperity, and good health and featured motifs from nature such as the moon and the cypress tree. Muslim girls often wore a *barracan*, a piece of cloth about two yards long that was wrapped around their bodies and drawn over their heads and shoulders. The barracan was originally made of coarse camlet but was later made in other, smoother fabrics, including heavy silk.

In addition to the hijab, other Islamic-based headdresses included face veils, or *mandeels*. In the winter, mandeels were made from thick wool; in the summer, women used thin muslin. Women also wore the *khmar*, a head covering and veil that hid everything but the eyes. During feasts, women in Bethlehem often wore black silk veils known as *shambars*.

Palestinian women's dress remained largely unchanged until the nineteenth century, when many began adopting Western dress. For women who continued to wear the tarha, European influence showed itself in new motifs, such as horses and peacocks. In some areas, highly decorative tarhas evolved, such as the *khirka* scarf from Ramallah and the *ghudfeh* scarf from Hebron. Both were intricately embroidered with red silk thread and had large panels of geometric and abstract shapes along the edges and in the center.

The war of 1948 prompted many Palestinians to flee to Lebanon, Jordan, and what became the West Bank and Gaza Strip. As refugees, it was difficult for Arab women to keep up the old ways. Although men continued to wear their kuffiyas, women found it increasingly awkward to wear their bulky tarhas and hijabs. Today, few Palestinian women wear traditional headdresses on a regular basis, although they do bring them out for festivals and religious occasions.

When it came time for me to leave Israel, getting out wasn't nearly as simple as coming in. The ticket agent at the airport took one look at my itinerary and sent for airport security. I was pulled to the side and asked—repeatedly—to explain why I was traveling to so many countries. My answer only led to more questions. "What was I going to write about Israel?" they asked. "Did I go into the Occupied Territories? What was I bringing into and taking out of each country?" Then I was taken into a room on the other side of the terminal, where agents systematically inspected every item in all of my bags. I was immensely relieved that I'd left my knife back in Paris.

After two hours of intense scrutiny, the agents repacked my luggage, more neatly than I had done myself, and sent me on my way. As I was leaving, agents had already begun to interrogate other hapless passengers. I wanted to wish them luck but was afraid the exchange would set off another series of red flags. I smiled to myself and ran as un-terrorist-like as I could to the boarding gate. My plane was about to take off for London, where I would remove my luggage tags and other proof that I'd been in Israel (my next destination, the United Arab Emirates, like many other Arab countries, doesn't admit people who've been in Israel) and board a different plane headed to Dubai.

United Arab Emirates

A basic requirement for entering the UAE is that one has to already live there or be invited by someone who does. Fortunately, I had a friend in the country, which was a good thing, because making new friends wasn't easy.

The professor at a technical college who had invited me introduced me to her friends, one of whom, a college student from Yemen, offered to take me out. We walked around a mall in Sharjah and sampled local perfumed oils, and then, back in the car, he surprised me by pulling into an unlit parking lot. It was dark outside, and from the road, the shadowy lot looked like an unpromising place to hang out. There were no buildings or signs, just a small kiosk and a dozen or so cars haphazardly parked between clusters of people sitting in lawn chairs. It wasn't until we pulled into the lot that I discovered what it really was: a roadside getaway to smoke *sheeshas*—three-foot-tall, freestanding aluminum water pipes. The lot attendant, a twenty-something man in jeans and a long-sleeved T-shirt, directed us to our parking space and took our order. (There was a choice of strawberry-, raspberry-, and apple-flavored tobaccos.)

After he brought over a single sheesha for us to share, I opened the car door to sit and smoke outside. But before I could shift my body to get out, the attendant told me to stay in the car: Only men could sit outside. "Yeah, right," I said. The car was stuffy, and the air outside was cool. If I was going to do this, I wanted to sit under the open sky. Unfortunately, what I wanted didn't matter. As a woman, if I wanted to smoke a sheesha in a parking lot, I apparently had no choice but to remain in the car. Then, my friend, taking advantage of his gender status, went out and lounged comfortably outside in a folding chair provided by the attendant. He snaked the pipe's tube and mouthpiece to me through the passenger-side window.

Everyone follows the rules in the UAE, a tiny, oil-rich country bordered by Oman, Saudi Arabia, and the Arabian (Persian) Gulf. Fearing deportation, my friend from Yemen, and hundreds of other expats, tend to follow the rules more closely than UAE citizens. There are two worlds in the UAE: that of the locals, and that of the foreign-

Page 102 and this page: In the UAE, men from Yemen, Oman, and from rural areas tend to wrap their head coverings like turbans. Page 103: In Dubai and other big cities, men tend to wear their *shumaghs* loose with *agals* to hold them in place. Many women wear all-covering *burkas*, as in this photograph (right) from the early 1900s.

ers, people brought in to teach, learn from, or provide services to the locals. Foreigners quickly learn that it is important to respect the country's customs, and clothes, which follow rules of tradition, and play an important role in those customs. When it comes to headgear, those rules help define whether people are locals or expats, and if they're expats, what country they come from.

It's not uncommon to see Arab men in Western suits. But many wear traditional clothing such as *dishdashes*, ankle-length tunics made of white cotton, silk, or wool, and head coverings worn with agals—similar to the kuffiyas among Palestinians. The *ghutrah*, a head covering made with white fabric, and the *shumagh*, a covering with a checkered pattern, are the two main choices. Most Arab women also wear Western clothes, but when in public they almost always cover their clothes with *abayas*—black outer robes that button up to the neck. On their heads, they wear modern headscarves or traditional hijabs and *shaliyas*—large squares of fabric used as headscarves. Who wears what is generally left up to each individual's personal taste and his or her adherence to Sharia. Men sometimes mix traditional head coverings with Western clothes, and local women are free to go outside with their hair uncovered, or even without their abayas if they choose. While I was there, I didn't see anyone who made that choice.

Before the advent of Islam in the seventh century, Bedouin and Arab women wore headscarves for practical reasons—to protect themselves from the desert heat and wind. With the rise of Islam, scarves took on the religious significance they have today. Between the Qur'an and the hadith, or narratives of what the Prophet Muhammad said and did, there are as many as thirteen verses that pertain to proper women's dress. Some detail when women should cover themselves (Sura 24:31), and why (Sura 33:59); another gives older women the option of covering a bit less (Sura 24:59).

Shumaghs can also be worn without *agals* and can be loosely tied in the back of the head.

For the first time, women began to hide the slope of their bosoms and secure scarves snugly over their hairline and ears and under the chin. In some regions, doing so not only became part of Sharia, but also part of *taqlid*, established Islamic

Suit jackets and turbans are common throughout the United Arab Emirates.

doctrine not to be questioned. As recently as the mid-1900s, in some villages in the Muslim world women who abandoned taqlid dress codes could be considered nonbelievers and doomed to damnation in this world and in the next. Today, only fundamentalists hold such strict views. Still, many local women continue to wear scarves and the larger shaliyas over their hairline.

For local women, scarves and shaliyas are also a fashion statement. They are often made of exquisite fabrics with a variety of textures and adorned with decorations that allow the wearer to strut her wealth, status, and individual style. High-end silk, cashmere, denim, and cotton scarves and shaliyas—some with ornate embroidery and hand-painted designs—are imported from all over the world and sold in specialized boutiques.

Some expats denounce the lavish styles that women of the UAE have popularized. A high-end boutique employee from Syria who spoke on the condition of anonymity insisted that "Muslim women should be modest." She said, "We're not supposed to draw attention to ourselves. Our scarves and abayas should be simple so we can appear modest. It's not enough to cover your hair when the fabric you cover it with is so lavish."

Most local women see it differently. Women who agreed to private interviews on the campus of Sheikh Zayed University said that as long as they behave appropriately, it does not go against their faith to be fashionable. "It's all in how you interpret the verse," one said. "I'm very attentive to how I dress. But I also like nice things. . . . I like to go shopping with my friends and find new styles. If there was something wrong with it, the stores wouldn't sell it, and my mother wouldn't let me buy it. There's nothing wrong with nice things," she added.

Muhammad's wives were the first to cover themselves for Islam. All except the first wife, who died before the edict was introduced, were ordered to wear a hijab, or "curtain," to "hide their beauty" from all men except those directly related to them or those too young or too old to be tempted by sex. That curtain took the form of a scarf, and the practice spread among Islam's elite as a sign of prestige and status. Noble ladies in Mecca and in other parts of the Middle East, such as Persia, wore veils and head coverings before Islam. Also, head coverings were already associated with a woman's status among some Assyrians and Babylonians. By the end of the eighth century, husbands and religious leaders throughout the Islamic world were demanding that women obey the scripture. But the verses in question are considered vague, and local Emirate women do not believe they restrict them from embracing contemporary fashions.

Emirate women usually start to cover their heads right after puberty. Putting on the traditional scarves and shaliyas is an occasion that officially marks the end of their girlish lifestyles. "When I was fourteen, my aunt told my mother that it was time," recounted one local woman. She explained, "My mother hadn't said anything to me yet, and I was glad. When they made me start, I hated it. It itched all the time and I felt like I couldn't breathe. Then I went to class and my teacher talked about the importance of wearing them. She said we were getting older and starting to develop. I finally understood, and never complained about it again."

Some girls make the decision on their own or form pacts with their friends at school. "Okay," they'll say to each other, "next Friday, we'll all come to school wearing shaliyas, right?" Women insist that the decision to wear shaliyas and headscarves is not forced upon them. "We want to wear them," said one woman. "It is a sign that we are women. When I was a little girl, I used to play dress-up with my mom's scarves. It was fun, and I couldn't wait to be old enough to wear them myself," she said.

Women also have a say in how the scarves are worn, or rather, how much of their "beauty" should be covered. Most city women only cover their hair, ears, and neck. Some, mostly rural women, wear veils and burqas to cover their faces. Others, mostly fundamentalists, also wear gloves to cover their hands.

At home, head coverings are always handled with care and respect. Women never toss their scarves on the floor or use them for anything but to wear on their heads. "It's not that they're sacred," said one woman, but she added, "Well, in a way, they are. They are a part of our religion, like our prayer beads and the Holy Qur'an. They shouldn't be mistreated." For this reason, old head coverings are never thrown away or converted into

If a woman is not wearing a full *burka*, she will shield her face from onlookers. Women rarely look strangers in the face, particularly ones with cameras.

Most men wear the *ghutrah* (left) and the *shumagh* (right) interchangeably, although *shumaghs* are more common in the winter because they are thicker and warmer.

rags. Instead, local women donate their old scarves and shaliyas to their female servants or to charitable organizations. And stylish Emirate women never use pins or brooches to hold their scarves and shaliyas in place. "Pins damage the fabric. It's much nicer if you can make a scarf stay without a pin. Not everybody can, or maybe they don't make the effort. But we do," the same woman explained.

In Islamic communities, men are just as responsible as women for maintaining a look of decency and modesty, which they achieve, in part, by wearing traditional clothing. At least two thousand years ago, men in the Arabian desert wore head coverings and early versions of the billowy dishdashes, which were easy to make and helped block the severe heat, wind gusts, and sandstorms. Later, the Prophet

Muhammad, who covered his head, taught that a person who wore a turban or other head covering could be protected from misguided evils.

The dimensions of men's head cloths in the UAE are specific. They start at 42 square inches and go up to 52 square inches, with intermediate sizes increasing in increments of 2 inches in length and width. There are four main styles. The most common head cloth in the UAE is the plain white cotton ghutrah, from the Arabic root *ghatar*, which means "to cover." The square fabric is folded diagonally into a triangle, then draped over the head with the fold across the forehead and the ends hanging down the back and shoulders. One or both corners are often flipped over the head. Men from Qatar often starch the sides so that they flare outward "like cobras," according to the running joke among other Arab men.

Emirate men generally wear thick cotton and wool shumaghs in the winter, or when they are out falconing in high altitudes. Shumaghs, from the Turkish word *yashmak*, which also means "to cover," are usually red and white or black and white checked. They are worn mainly by the Saudis. Other head cloths, such as the kuffiya popular among Palestinians, Jordanians, and the Lebanese, are also checked, or have thick and thin brown, red, black, or green stripes along the edges. Paisley cloths wrapped into compact turbans are favored among Omani and Yemeni men. To help keep the head cloths in place, men wear white cotton skullcaps, or *taqiyyas*, underneath, and agals on top.

I realized after I left that none of the men I'd been introduced to had worn traditional dress when they hung out with me. That seemed odd, and I wondered if it was because I'm a westerner and had worn Western clothes, or if it was their usual practice. Perhaps they didn't want me to feel uncomfortable. Or maybe they would have felt uncomfortable in traditional dress when I was with them. Men in the UAE react to women's clothes more than they react to women. If I had worn shaliyas and other Islamic dress while in Dubai, I'm sure I would have been treated differently. For one thing, I never would have been invited to smoke sheeshas that night. And when I was at the beach or parked along the road for a rest with the women I'd met, we would have been expected to remain covered, no matter what the weather. We would not have been able to walk freely around the areas where men sat without their shirts. My dress had determined how I was treated by men my age. I'm glad that I had decided to stick to Western clothing. It had allowed me to explore otherwise off-limits aspects of the UAE.

India

While I was in India, my senses remained on full alert. They had to.

Every pursuit of a different turban led to a grand adventure that was more amazing than the one before. For example, twenty minutes into a drive from Jaipur, in eastern Rajasthan, to the 400-year-old Samode Palace two hours to the north, I had to stop the car for something unexpected on the side of the road: an encampment of what the locals call "gypsies." All the men were gone, leaving three women and a dozen children to greet me at the edge of their circle of tents. The two oldest boys, both in their teens, put themselves in charge and did all the talking.

They and the other children were dressed in Western clothes. The women were in traditional Indian dress: long, pleated skirts, or *ghagras*; short-sleeved tops, or *cholis*; and thin, cotton *dupattas*, or scarves draped over their heads. Everyone was covered with dust, but the women's yellow, fuchsia, red, green, and blue dupattas were still eye-poppingly bright. On their foreheads were smears of soot and vermilion, and embedded in their front teeth were tiny pieces of colored glass. I immediately recognized the smears, or *tilakas*, as common marks of Hinduism. The glass was new to me, although the adornment is common in many parts of rural India. Each piece of glass represents a different precious stone and is believed to protect one of the nine *chakras*—or spiritual centers—in the body. I stayed for a while in their off-road community, where large cooking pots hovered over open flames, a baby slept in a hammock of rags near

Page 110: A Sikh in his *pagri* in Amritsar, Punjab. Page 111: Gypsies in *dupattas* and a merchant in a turban, both from small villages north of Jaipur, Rajasthan.
This page: The colored glass pieces embedded in this Hindu woman's teeth are believed to protect her *chokras*.

the fire, and the pubescent boys took turns sneaking up and sticking their hands in my pockets.

Standing by me was Raj, a doe-eyed shop owner from Jaipur who had borrowed his father's car to drive me around. Raj sells woodblock and batik print blankets near the Surabhi turban museum in Jaipur's old quarter. We had met the day before, when he helped settle a nasty dispute between me and a rickshaw driver.

Raj and I left the encampment before the baby woke up, bought some Hindi music for the journey, and were halfway to the palace when we stopped again. An old man with thick glasses and a round, hypertrophic turban was walking down a path with his cow. At the same time, a man with a colorful turban riding a beautiful mare was approaching us in a wedding procession that took up over half the road. I knew I had to take some pictures. By the time Raj stopped the car and I ran back to the old man, however, he had already veered away from his emaciated cow to squat and relieve himself. I felt awkward waiting, but I couldn't very well leave, either. Knowing that every village in Rajasthan has its own characteristic turban, and that a new village might be around the next bend, I couldn't risk never seeing this one again—a turban made from two pieces of cotton, one white and the other black and white checked, tied on top of one another. Trying not to be too obvious, I turned around to watch the wedding party. Dozens of people flanked a rather somber groom-to-be who wore a dark gray suit and an ill-matched, but truly spectacular, turban. The turban, or *safa* in Hindi, had bands of smooth red, blue, and yellow silk sewn together and a long, red tail hanging down one side. The groom's horse was decorated with red, yellow, and green plastic flowers and matching streamers.

I must have looked odd standing there on the path with my camera and a cow, because people in the procession were staring. Someone finally picked up on what was happening. Word spread, and the entire procession started laughing. The old man must have heard their jeers, because he quickly straightened himself up and shuffled toward me. He hesitated, and I thought he was pausing for the camera. Evidently, I was wrong. All of a sudden, he started screaming at me, brandishing his cane wildly in the air. I ran toward the car just as Raj was backing it up toward me. We sped off into the hills, a perfect getaway.

The rest of the day, and every day in India before and after, was filled with exotic sights, strange adventures, and wondrous headwraps. Rajasthan, the vast, arid state in northwestern India, promised the greatest variety, as it is famous for having engineered more than 1,000 different turban styles. From the ninth to the twelfth centuries, during the days of the Rajputs—mainly Hindus of the warrior caste—turbans, or safas, were the region's quintessential accessory. Color-coded for the climate, *safas* were usually bright red, orange, sunshine yellow, and purple in dry, barren areas, and more muted lavenders, grays, light blues, and light browns in lush, green areas. Men who could afford it sported different colors for each season. Mainly worn for protection from the sun, the turbans were often unwound and the fabric used to hobble animals, lower buckets into wells, dry off with, carry things in, or cover up with by wrapping the fabric around the waist and between the legs like a pair of pants.

On a road in rural Rajasthan, I crossed paths with this man (and his cow) and this groom (and his horse), both wearing distinctive turbans.

At least eighty safa styles are on display in a room of the Surabhi Museum and Restaurant in Jaipur. The owner and curator, Dharam Vir Singh, said he created the museum in 1999 because he feared turbans were becoming extinct. "Wrapping them

is a lost art. In some villages, only one person remembers how they're supposed to be done," he said during my tour of the museum. I was thrilled to examine the variety of styles, all neatly aligned on shelves behind glass cases. "At first, I collected the styles I liked and used them as decoration in my restaurant. Then as I collected more, I decided to start a museum," he explained.

Singh said he sent teams of people all over Rajasthan to document traditional styles. "We took white or gray fabric and asked the local people in each village to dye it according to their custom. Then we asked an elder to tie it, which he usually did around a team member's head. After that, we pinned it, put it in a box, and returned to Jaipur." Some turbans were either too big for a box or too sensitive to remove from the men's heads and had to be worn home on the train. "The men were often ridiculed for traveling with a strange turban," Singh said.

As early as the fourth century, the quality and shape of a man's safa was an indicator of his caste and status. By the time of the Rajputs, each village had a separate safa for musicians, merchants, farmers, and rulers. "In some villages, the richest businessman in the village had his own safa style," said Singh.

Most Rajputan safas were made from nine meters of fabric, hand woven and hemmed by the women in each household. Some styles were round and plump; others were narrow and tubular. Some were wrapped with the stiff and crinkly fabric typical of the Rajputs, and others were made with woven cotton or spun silk. For the truly wealthy, prized turbans were made from forty-four meters of fabric and took at

A jeweler in Jaipur (top) and a sheep-herder of the nomadic Rabari tribe in the state of Gujarat (bottom) wear their *safas* proudly. At right, a selection of turbans displayed at the Surabhi Museum and Restaurant in Jaipur.

least two hours to wrap. A man who wore such an elaborate turban usually wore the same one without unraveling it for at least two weeks at a time.

Whether made from silk or from rags, a man's safa became a symbol of his prestige. It was said that a person's status could be judged from three things: *raftar, dastar,* and *guftar. Raftar* meant his mannerisms and body language. *Dastar* was another term for turban. *Guftar* meant his manner of speaking. For many men throughout India, turbans were the foundation of their identity. To remove a turban from a man's head was considered the ultimate insult.

A turning point in the connection between men and their turbans came in the 1400s with the rise of the Mughals, Muslim invaders from Persia and Afghanistan. By the late sixteenth century, Mughals ruled as far north as Kashmir and as far south as the Deccan. At that time, Muslims from the Ottomans to the Moors had already claimed turbans as the headdress of Islam and routinely ruled that only Muslims could wear them, or that only Muslims could wear certain colors and styles. The Mughals were no different. They decreed that, with the exception of the Rajputs, non-Muslims could not wear turbans, except while tilling the fields. They also ruled that non-Muslims could not ride horses into cities, carry weapons, or grow mustaches and beards.

Among those rejecting the Mughals' policies was a growing number of men in the north who believed that equality and love should exist for everyone. These men, known as Sikhs, considered headwraps to be a birthright that couldn't be taken away. Moreover, they considered the turban—or *pagri,* another term for turban used throughout India—to be an integral part of their dress.

The Sikh religion began in the Punjab region of northern India in the late 1400s with Nanak Dev. The son of Hindu parents, Guru Nanak denounced the divisions of caste and rank and preached a philosophy of one God, with tolerance and acceptance of all. As the religion took root, so did the number of men who continued to wear turbans.

By the late 1600s, Mughal emperors had killed two Sikh gurus and led a number of campaigns against Sikhs. In 1699, Gobind Singh, the tenth guru, initiated a new order of Sikhs and began a campaign to systematically fight Mughal authority. He called for Sikhs to be baptized and adopt five *kakars,* or symbolic practices that had to do with elements of the Sikh's *bana,* personal appearance. One of these was to keep

Top: An officer in his *pagri* directs traffic on the road to Amritsar. Bottom: This *nihang* wears the Sikh symbol pinned to the front of his *pagri.*

their hair in the natural form in which God had created it. This meant that men and women shouldn't cut or trim their hair. The turban, of course, became a sensible tool for maintaining long hair, which men usually tied into a topknot, or bun, first, then wrapped with cloth.

With so much history, I had to go north and interview Sikhs myself. In the former industrial town of Ludhiana, I stayed with a tax accountant named Joginder Singh and his family, all of whom spoke perfect English and eagerly shared a great deal about Sikh culture. Mrs. Singh had the cook prepare a unique Punjabi dish at every meal, and she looked me over daily with a mother's eye to make sure I was wearing my *salwar kameez* (traditional long tunic and pants with matching *chuni,* or scarf) properly. Mr. Singh made sure I understood the pride and attention that a Sikh puts into wrapping and maintaining his pagri. Their eldest son, Rabinder, handled all the other introductions, translations, and sightseeing, making sure I was exposed to the whole range and variety of Sikh turbans.

Above: Joginder Singh, my host in Ludhiana, with his granddaughter. His turban was wrapped meticulously every morning in a style worn by most Sikh men in the Punjab. Below: Boys wear the *patka* until they are ready for the *pagri.*

Pagri styles have changed over the centuries but have maintained a cohesive look among most men of a generation. The modern pagri has an angled front, with layers of crisp folds on the sides. In the Punjab, traffic police wear decorative pagris with pleated fans sticking up from one side. In Amritsar, an order of warrior Sikhs known as *nihangs,* as well as some older men, wear the royal blue pagri of eighteenth-century Sikh soldiers.

Boys begin wearing the topknot when they're as young as two years old and usually cover it with a cotton or nylon *patka.* Patkas are like starter turbans, only they don't require any wrapping around the head. The cloth is placed over the hairline, the two front ends are tied in the back, and the two back ends are tied around the hair in a knot—or bun—at the top. Boys grow up watching their fathers tie their pagris. In a special coming-of-age ceremony held between the ages of seven and fourteen called the *dastar bandhi,* a Sikh boy puts on his first pagri, but afterward, he will go back to wearing the patka. There's no mandatory age when a young Sikh has to begin wearing a full turban, although most begin in their late teens. It's a big decision. Pagri cloth is generally five to six meters long and one meter wide. The patkas, by comparison, measure only about two and a half feet square. Young

men have to get used to wearing the weight of more cloth and have to be willing to devote the time that is needed to wrap the pagri properly. "You can tell when a man takes his time to wrap his turban," said Mr. Singh, who sits in front of his bedroom mirror every morning to tie his headdress. "There's no excuse for a sloppy turban."

A Hindu woman in Jodhpur.

To help me truly understand the Sikh community and its history, Rabinder drove me north, to Amritsar. There, we visited the Golden Temple, a sort of Vatican City for Sikhs. To enter, I had to first store my shoes in an outside shoe-check. Then I walked across the cold concrete toward the main entrance and stepped into a shallow footbath of even colder water. Rabinder did the same, and with my chuni covering my hair, we walked in together.

The Golden Temple sits in the middle of a lake across a marble bridge. When we visited, hundreds of people were there, but the entire campus was so large that it never seemed crowded. We walked around the lake, passing people taking a dip, reading, and praying. Before we entered the temple, I bought a plate of *krah prashad* (a mixture of whole-wheat flour or semolina, sugar, butter, and water) to use as a symbolic offering. Inside, the two-story temple was spectacular. The huge Sikh Holy Book, Guru Granth Sahib, rested on a pedestal covered with a red velvet blanket. The walls, floors, and ceiling of the *gurudwara,* or house of worship, were gilded, painted with complex floral designs, or covered with tapestry. We stayed for an hour listening to hymns from Guru Granth Sahib by a small chorus, or *ragis.*

Later, we drove around Amritsar visiting smaller gurdwaras and different Sikh orders. We returned to Ludhiana before sunset just in time to get some sleep and be ready for my next adventure: a traditional Indian wedding. Rabinder's cousin was to be married, and I was invited to attend. I packed an overnight bag with two lovely salwar kameezes that Mrs. Singh had helped me pick out. (She also had Rabinder promise to help me find something dressier than my hiking boots.) The wedding was in Chandigarh, about two hours east of Ludhiana. We arrived the night before the wedding, just in time to watch the bride get her hands and feet adorned with henna. The next day, the wedding had to take place at an auspicious hour determined by the *purohit,* or priest. (The groom was Hindu, so the wedding had elements of the two religions.) It was declared that nuptials would take place at 1:00 the following morning, so the festivities began in the early evening with an immense feast and toasts. All of the Sikh men wore neatly wrapped pagris, and the groom's close relatives wore

Rajputan-style safas. Most of today's ceremonial safas are stitched into hats and sold or rented ready-to-wear for each occasion. Usually, I could tell the difference, but it didn't matter. To me, they were all gorgeous, in their bright colors and long, decorative tails.

The bride wore a light pink and silver chuni over her head, just behind her hairline. When the wedding ceremony began, she sat on the floor with her chuni smoothed out around her, so that it rested like the train of a gown. I also wore a chuni, as did the other women. I took my cue from Mrs. Singh on how to elegantly keep it on my head, although I must admit it fell to my shoulders quite frequently. Like women in the UAE, Indian women rarely use pins or other devices to hold their dupattas and chunis in place. Fortunately, losing my scarf to gravity wasn't a social or religious problem that I had to be concerned about. But I came to view it as a cultural blunder that I was determined to get right before I left the country. Good thing for me, I had three weeks to practice.

Nepal

It was splendid chaos. To the left and right of me, vendors were hawking everything from multicolored knit scarves to intricate, gold inlaid tikal paintings, handmade paper lamps, and silver jewelry with opal, turquoise, or lapis lazuli stones. Behind me was more of the same, and up ahead, it continued. I was on Indra Chowk street, a main thoroughfare in the heart of Kathmandu. Souvenir shops were overflowing with four-inch Buddha statues, miniature wooden temples, and calendars with spectacular shots of the Himalayas, which, by the way, emblazoned the distant skyline.

In the middle of it all, standing right in front of me, was a man who made everything else disappear. He was dressed in a ruby red, long-sleeved tunic; bright red, brown, and white beads; a deep wine-colored wool blanket; and a dusty rose turban. Adjusting my ocular senses to get past all of those shades of red, I realized I was standing in front of the only man in Kathmandu that I'd seen wearing a turban. He was dressed like a *sadhu*, or Hindu holy man. Sort of. He had the markings on his forehead that traditionally denote a sadhu's sect, and his hand gestures and warm smile seemed to emanate the peaceful spirit of a holy man. But his tunic threw me. Sadhus generally try to reach enlightenment through intense sacrifice. This first and foremost means giving up sex. Beyond that, many also relinquish all family ties and material wealth, including clothes. Most wear only a blanket and a turban, or even the forgo the turban. Some don't even cover up with a blanket, preferring instead to go naked. Still, every sect is different, and I learned later on that some sects prescribe tunics.

Page 120: The *Sadhu* who blessed me in Kathmandu. Page 121: (left to right) *Sadhus* of different sects wear different *safas*; a curious onlooker in a simple gauze head cloth.
This page, right: *Sadhus* on their way to prayer. Below: a *sadui*.

Some also prescribe turbans. Turbans, or safas, allow sadhus to easily maintain their long locks. Once a man, or woman (Hindu holy women are called *sadhvis*), decides to pursue a path of enlightenment, he or she renounces the world to focus entirely on the Higher Reality that sadhus believe lies beyond physical existence. Sadhus stop cutting their hair in order to emulate Shiva, the Hindu god of destruction, whose supernatural powers were believed to stem from his long hair. Turbans offer a simple convenience in a lifestyle that has few luxuries. Sadhus also cover themselves with ash as a symbolic acknowledgment of death and rebirth. They eat only simple foods, and little of that. Most are very lean, not at all like the man I met, who looked remarkably robust. Sadhus are also known to be extremely gentle and soft-spoken. To his credit, the man I met was both of those.

We stood on Indra Chowk street for just a few moments. He didn't speak English and was clearly on his way to somewhere else. Still, he took a moment to stay with me. He motioned his right hand up and down and said a few words I didn't understand. Then he smudged some juice from a red rose petal on my forehead and sprinkled a handful of petals into my hair. After that, he closed his eyes, bowed his head, then looked up at me and smiled. I smiled back. In that moment, I felt warm and relaxed. I gave him a few coins and thanked him for the blessing.

That was my last day in Nepal, and it was the only turban I saw there. Headwraps are rare in Nepal. Most men wear small, round caps if they wear a head covering at all. Women often cover their heads with a dupatta or a shawl when in the presence of elders. Turbans are more popular among ethnic groups high in the Himalayan Mountains. I did not visit them, but I was told that along with pointed, knit caps and Tibetan-style bronze helmets, many indigenous mountain tribes wear headwraps. Among them are the Rai people in northeastern Nepal. Neither Hindu nor Buddhist, they have their own deities and beliefs. They also have a unique form of dress that, for women, includes a broad, bulky headdress. They wrap the fabric from the back to the front, then flip the excess material over their heads and leave it to hang down their backs.

Looking back, I believe my sadhu and his momentary presence were meant to be. Until that moment, I wasn't sure if the custom of wearing turbans had died out in Kathmandu. But then he appeared, and his simple, dusty rose safa with its loose folds and soft curves erased a week of self-doubt. When he walked away, I was left standing alone in the center of the street, surrounded by paper lamps and Buddha statues. I smiled at how easy it was to dismiss such worldly wares while he was with me, and how I was immediately aware of them again once he left. I was also distinctly aware of the time. I had to get back to the hotel and pack.

Asia / South Pacific

China

In Chinese, *mah jong means "sparrow,"* but to the people who play the game, it means high stakes gambling. I didn't know this when I first walked into the Hong Kong Mah Jong Company in Wan Chai, a district of Hong Kong made popular in Richard Mason's book *The World of Suzie Wong* (1957). Private mah jong parlors like the Hong Kong Mah Jong Company are exclusive. They allow serious players only and don't usually welcome spectators. They are reputedly run by the Chinese mafia, and in some parts of China they operate illegally. Most don't have windows, and many only advertise with a small plaque with the establishment's name etched in Chinese characters outside the door. Almost all of them have a plainclothes guard posted at the entrance.

From the outer vestibule of the parlor, I could hear the high-pitched clatter of hundreds of tiles being slammed onto tabletops. One game of mah jong has 144 domino-like tiles, and it sounded like a dozen games were being played all at once. I begged the guard to let me in, and to my surprise, he did. (I'd gone to two other mah jong parlors, and they both had rejected me.) When I opened the double wooden doors to the game room, I hesitated for a moment. The room, no bigger than an average-sized living room, was filled with more cigarette smoke than oxygen, and more people than any fire code would allow. Ten, maybe fifteen tables were crowded into three or four rows, with four people playing a game at each table. Most were men, a few were women. An employee guarding the room nodded for me to stay put near one of the tables by the door. I wasn't allowed to take pictures, or to stay for very long. I'd expected a lot of verbal sparring, like in the dominoes games I'd played in college. But no one said a word. People just smoked cigarettes and silently played one game after another. All the noise came from the cream-colored tiles, each one decorated with an animal on one half and a green or red Chinese character on the other. The game is played a little like rummy, but I couldn't figure out the rules. I was dying to ask someone. But I had to be grateful that I was even there and didn't want to push my luck.

Skimming the surface of China's underworld was the last thing I had expected to do in Asia. With the bilingual safety net of Hong Kong as my base, I expected to spend a week on Hainan Island in the South China Sea. There, I believed I'd find an ethnic group that wears traditional headwraps. But the minute I arrived in Hong Kong, nothing went according to plan, and I never got further than a high-rise apartment complex in Kowloon, Hong Kong. It was there, in the cluttered three-bed-room home of my host family, that I was first told that the people I was looking for didn't exist. Other people I asked said the same thing.

I was sure they were wrong, but in the end, I decided to cancel my plans. I stayed in Hong Kong for two days. It wasn't until after I left that my suspicions were confirmed. There are more than fifty-five minority nationalities living in China, some of whom reside on Hainan Island. In all, they wear more than 300 headdress styles,

Page 126: A Side Comb Miao man and woman outside the door of their home in Long Dong village, Guangxi Province; Page 127, left to right: Members of a reception committee for visiting officials in Ninglang County, Yunna Province. The woman on the left is Na and the other two are Nuosu from Ninglang; An elderly Buyei woman in Bi Ke village, Guizhou Province. This page: In Gao Zhai village, Miao men perform a dance in which they pretend to stir sticky rice.

from wrapped turbans to beaded caps and headbands. I'd left when I should have stayed and then spent months scrambling to learn what I should have seen.

Some minorities in China are immigrant ethnic groups, such as the Uzbeks, Russians, and Koreans. Others are indigenous peoples such as the Yi, the Jingpos, and the Lahu. They all have distinctive cultures, languages, and architectural styles. Most are looked down upon by the Han, China's majority ethnic group. For centuries, the Han considered the minorities barbarians.

All of the minority nationalities are as different as the climates they live in. The Nuosu, a subgroup of the Yi, live in a region east of the Tibetan highlands that they call "Nimu"; most Chinese call it "Liangshan." Their clothing styles correspond to three regional subdivisions. In northern Liangshan, men wear "big trouser legs." That is, their pant legs are exceptionally wide, sometimes as wide as a woman's pleated skirt. In central Liangshan, men wear "medium trouser legs"; and in the south, they wear "small trouser legs," or rather, their pant legs are tapered at the ankles.

To learn more, I reached out to Stevan Harrell, a professor in the Asian studies department at the University of Washington. Throughout the Nuosu homeland, which Harrell described as cold and barren, everyone wears thick capes, or *carwas*, layers of clothes, and some type of tribal hat or headwrap. Men traditionally wear black cotton turbans. They twist the ends of their turbans into a stiff hero's horn that

Above: A young Nuosu girl stands outside her home.
Left: Nuosu women from Yanyuan dressed for a wedding. They wear extra scarves and yarn to protect them against the cold.

Right: A Nuosu man in his hero's horn turban.

pokes out from the side, front, top, or back of their turbans. Whether young or old, they always pay particular attention to the appearance of their hero's horns.

Adult women with no children wear black or red cotton headdresses with elaborate embroidery and cross-stitching. They begin wearing them in their late teens, after a coming-of-age ceremony called *shahla ge*, or "changing the skirt." As part of the ceremony, they restyle their single braid of hair into two braids and for the first time tie their hair up in a traditional headdress, or *uofa*. Styles vary from rounded turbans to symmetrical, awning-shaped headdresses. They slope upward to a broad peak at the top, with the sides

of the fabric hanging loose to their shoulders. Some uofas are made from layers of folded fabric placed in a semicircle on the forehead like a visor. To keep their headdresses secure, women often tie yarn, strips of fabric, or strings of beads around them. Like the men's hero's horns, the women's uofas are a focus of much attention. A woman wears her uofa every day, inside the house and out, as a sign of her maturity, generally until she has her first child. She then replaces it with a hat, or *uoly*.

Throughout China, most minority groups are separated by di-

Left: Young Bouyei girls welcome visitors to the village.
Below: A Side Comb Miao woman and baby. The baby's hat is fringed with protective metal buddhas.

alects, and many subgroups are further divided by location, dress, and other factors. Each group has its own costume identity. The head covering plays an important part. In many minority groups, headwraps reflect a stage in a person's life, a family's wealth, or a woman's skill as a weaver and, therefore, her suitability as a wife.

To learn more, I turned to Pamela Cross, a textile collector in England who has focused on the way textiles are used to express identity, life milestones, and wealth. "In China, textiles can act as signposts to migration," she said, "particularly in the southwest where minority groups were pushed by the Han into remote highland areas in China, Vietnam, Thailand, and Laos." Cross's research has focused primarily on two groups: the Side Comb Miao people in the Long Dong village of Guangxi province and the Bouyei people in Bi Ke village in Guizhou province.

The Side Comb Miao (who call themselves "Hmangh"—or Hmong—which means "cotton clothes") migrated to the highest and most inhospitable lands, where they developed headdress styles that were both attractive and warm. Married women among the Miao wear heavy swathes of black fabric—today velvet or corduroy bought

in the market—secured by bands of white or blue over their hair, which is twisted into a knot at the side and secured by a wooden comb.

In contrast, the Bouyei live at lower altitudes in the more fertile river valleys. Their women wear bright white or striped indigo turbans, which they weave themselves. These are starched and elaborately folded and tied for festivals or celebrations. Both the Side Comb Miao and the Bouyei are famous for their skill in weaving and embroidery.

The Han have a sporadic history with turbans. As early as 200 B.C., ribbons were used to contain men's hair in a bun on top of the head. Many of the soldiers in the vast army of terra-cotta warriors from that period wore ribbons like this. At least since the third century A.D., many Chinese considered it uncivilized to go out without something on one's head, and men throughout the countryside often wore turbans. In his book *Chinese Civilization* (1930), Marcel Granet explained that at that time, nobles at court wore different headdresses "in times of mourning, of abstinence, or disgrace, when one [was] dealing with business and when one [was] resting." According to Granet, it was said that a man "does not die unless [his] head-dress is set well upon [his] head." In 1178, a school code of practices and procedures for

Above: A Side Comb Miao woman carries bamboo poles back to her village. Below: The "liang pa t'ou erh" or "two handle headdress" is still worn by some Chinese stage actresses as well as by some rural Manchus on New Year's Day.

young boys included the long established norm of binding their hair when getting dressed. And during the Tang period, *Analects for Women*, a text based on Confucian teachings, insisted that if a woman had to go outside, she should cover her face.

During the Ming Dynasty (1368–1644), the scholar Qian Gu-xun wrote that women "tied their hair in a bun, bounded with a white cloth." Around 1835, during the reign of Tsu Hsi, the Empress Dowager of the Qing Dynasty, court women began draping satin cloth over a centuries-old Manchu hairstyle. In the *liang pa t'ou erh*, or "two handle headdress," hair (then hair plus hairpieces, and later hair plus satin or silk in a much higher and more pronounced version) was built up over a wire framework, with the gilded, rounded ends of the metal protruding on both sides. It was often decorated with jewelry, silk flowers, and scarlet tassels.

From 1898 to 1900, a secret society of men from Shandong province known as the Fists of Righteous Harmony made headwraps a distinctive part of the Empress Dowager's legacy. Known as

Boxers by foreigners because they used martial arts, the men fought to save the Qing Dynasty in uniforms that included bright red turbans. In recounting the eight-week Boxer Uprising beginning in June 1900, an English writer wrote that their turbans could be seen from at least twenty yards away. Tsu Hsi died in 1908, and the Qing Dynasty collapsed three years later.

After that, dress styles changed dramatically, reflecting a number of social and political developments. By the mid-1900s, China's indigenous dress and minority traditions were threatened as ethnic minorities were forced to embrace mainstream Chinese culture. In 1956, Communists introduced reforms intended to put China on the road to modernization. They established county governments and built schools, roads, and cities where there were once only meeting houses, trails, and small markets. In 1966, the newly established People's Republic of China initiated a Cultural Revolution, seeking to eliminate what the Communist government, especially Mao Tse-tung, considered the barbaric traditions of minority populations. Ethnic clothes were considered backward, and people were forced to abandon them.

The Cultural Revolution lasted for ten years. After it was over, the Nuosu, the Miao, and other groups underwent a cultural renaissance. Their handmade musical instruments and traditional dress reemerged and now coexist with battery-operated radios and modern, store-bought clothes. The hero's horn of Nuosu men has almost disappeared. Only a few of the elders, and a few intellectuals trying to reconstruct forgotten traditions, still wear it. Other Nuosu men have begun wearing turbans made from pink floral bath towels, which are cheaper and easier to wrap and wash.

The people of Hong Kong were almost completely removed from the monumental changes taking place in mainland China. By initially choosing to enter China through Hong Kong instead of Beijing, I unwittingly chose cosmopolitanism over tradition. That's not to say that my two days in Hong Kong were all bad. In addition to the mah jong parlors, I went to tea ceremonies, galleries, and high-end shopping malls. But best of all, back in the apartment in Kowloon, my host mother fixed me toasted peanut butter and sliced-apple sandwiches for breakfast and lunch. Now how could I not love that?

Above: Tea masters traditionally wore silk ribbons tied around braided buns. Below: Han men traditionally wore headwraps, as depicted in this 10th-century illustration of a hunting party.

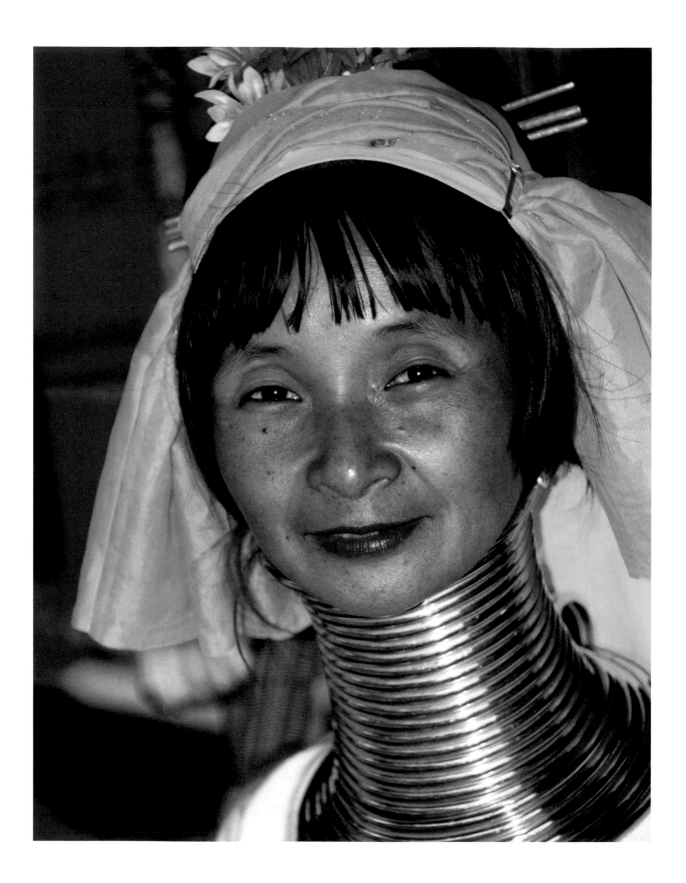

Thailand

No one likes to be stared at. So when my tour group arrived in a mountain village in northern Thailand to see the Padaung, or Longneck people, I understood why one little girl with lime and peach taffeta hair ribbons never smiled. The fourteen brass rings that elongated her neck made her a popular tourist attraction. She knew it, and I could tell she didn't like it.

Still, there we were, one of a dozen groups that comes and goes every day. We didn't seem to bother the older girls as much, and the adult women seemed downright tickled to have another vanload of gawkers. They smiled and posed for photographs in the muddy center of a U-shaped market of bamboo stalls with grass roofs and shelves of handcrafted bags, pillowcases, textiles, and key chains. The women hoped that after the tourists took all the pictures they wanted, they would look around and buy something. According to my guide, who spoke with some of the villagers, no one in the group before us had bought anything. And if the pursed lips of the bored little girl were any indication, no one in my group was likely to buy anything either.

According to legend, the neck rings, as well as rings on the women's legs, helped protect the women from tigers that used to attack their villages. The tigers, apparently, went for the neck and extremities. "The men were able to fight back, but the women were too weak," explained my tour guide. Today, the tigers are endangered, but the neck and leg rings are

Previous spread (left to right): A Padaung woman ties her hair in neon-colored ribbons to keep it from getting tangled in her neck rings; a Northern Thai in a modern version of 14th-century Lanna kingdom dress; a Padaung girl; a Lahu woman near her home in Chiang Mai.

This page: Ceremonial headdresses worn by a young Hmong girl (left) and a Karen woman (right) in separate villages around Chiang Mai. Opposite page: Karen women and other Chao Khao in northern Thailand wrap towels around their heads for creative everyday styles.

still a part of the heritage of the Padaung. Five oversized neck rings are first put on little girls when they're five years old. As the girls grow older, the rings begin to press down on their collar bones and compress their ribcages. Their necks become elongated, making space for more rings. By the time they're adults, women can fit as many as twenty-six rings around their necks. They pin their hair up into a bun with three or four chopsticks to keep it from getting snagged between the rings, then decorate it with neon pink, yellow, blue, and green ribbons and lace.

The Padaung are one of many Chao Khao tribes on Thailand's tourist trail. The Chao Khao, a term usually translated as "mountain people" or "hill tribes" but that literally means "them people," are not Thai. Over the centuries, they immigrated to Thailand from rural parts of Burma, Laos, and China. Each tribe has its own language, dress, religion, and culture. Most villages that are accessible to tourists are known as *nikhoms*, resettlement villages established by the Thai government to help the Chao Khao assimilate into Thai society. Being open for tourism and profiting from it are two different things, however, and the Padaung women aren't as aggressive as other Chao Khao. For one thing, they don't charge people for taking photographs of them. Akha women, who wear red knit caps layered with dangling silver coins, do. Padaung women do not insist that a person buy something expensive in exchange for a photograph, either. Mien women, who wear dark indigo costumes with red faux-fur collars and turbans made from wide strips of indigo fabric, do. Instead, Padaung women rely on the tour guides to make a general plea for support, and they have a small wood donation box nailed at eye-level to a tree on the only path out.

For the Padaung, Yao, Akha, and other Chao Khao, headdresses are an important part of their identity. In the six largest ethnic groups—the Hmong, Yao, Akha, Lahu, Lisu, and Karen—all of the women and some men wear distinctive hats or headwraps. They rarely go outside without their heads covered, and they all can be closely identified by the color and shape of their headdresses. Every Karen woman, for example, has two headwraps. For special occasions, there is a crimson red and white handwoven textile with long red fringes that is either wound like a turban or partially folded and placed on the head so that a curtain of fabric hangs over the nape of the neck. On regular days, a rectangle of white or pink cotton cloth, almost one meter wide, is wrapped once or twice around the head, then the excess is flipped up from the forehead to the back and left to hang loose over the shoulders. Often a young woman decorates her headdress with a beaded headband with brightly colored pompoms.

For festive occasions, Lisu women wear black turbans. Girls wrap strips of inexpensive black cloth into neat, tightly wound reels, then cover the reels with wider strips of good

quality black cloth (sometimes velvet). For a splash of color, they then attach long strands of yellow, blue, pink, and red yarn by wrapping the collective strands over one side, under the front of the turban, and back over the other side. The portion passing across the front of the turban is strung with glass beads and embellished with pompoms. The rest of the yarn is spread out over the back of the turban and hangs to the shoulders. Older Lisu women wear unembellished black turbans loosely wound around their heads. For everyday use, most women wrap bath towels around their heads.

Among the Lahu, most men and women wear small black turbans, although in some subgroups, they may wear large white turbans with layers of twists and tucks or small turbans with red, white, and black stripes. For New Year's festivities, Lahu Nyi men wear turbans made from two yards each of red, black, and white cloth. Lahu Shi headmen wear pink silk turbans. Unmarried Lahu Shi women decorate their turbans with strips of brightly colored cloth, buttons, beads, and coins.

Yao women take time to embroider red, blue, yellow, green, and white geometric designs on strips of black cloth, then wrap their

Top: A Lisu woman wears a hand-crafted, layered headdress. Bottom: A Yao woman wears an embroidered black cloth wrapped into a turban.

turbans so the embroidery is visible. Depending on the woman and her subgroup, the embroidery may be at the end of the fabric and stick upward through the wide, circular folds of the turban. If the embroidery is in the center of the cloth, then it's always visible as an outside layer of the wound fabric. Yao priests wear elaborate red headdresses that begin like closely wound turbans, then—with ribbons, embroidered panels, and fringes—end up as eight-inch-high headpieces with wide strips of fabric that hang down the back.

On New Year's, Hmong women wear layered, peaked headwraps made from strips of black and white checked fabric. Girls use fourteen or fifteen strips, and married women use anywhere from twenty to fifty.

There are other headwraps within the Chao Khao community, but even without the Chao Khao, northern Thailand has a rich, colorful tradition of turbans. The people of ancient Lan Na, a collection of northern territory kingdoms from the 1300s to the 1550s, are remembered for their stylish turbans, known as *jao nage* for women and *jao nay* for men in the northern Thai language. Worn mostly by royalty, and by common people for special occasions, these turbans were short and round, made from one or two pieces of fine cotton or silk fabric, and decorated with plumes or gold ornaments. Even after the fall of Lan Na, turbans continued to be worn among descendants of Lan Na culture. A photo from 1896 of the king of Muang Sing and his cortege, originally published in *Travels in Laos: The Fate of Sip Song Pana and Muong Sing* (1898) by E. Lefevre, shows everyone wearing turbans. The look is frequently recreated in specialty photo studios in Chiang Mai, where men and women change into luxurious Thai silk clothes and put on elaborate versions of the ancient turbans, then go home with 5x7 prints for posterity.

The photographs reminded me that I had pictures of my own that needed to be developed. When I got to Bangkok, that's the first thing I did. I wish I hadn't. The photo lab destroyed a roll of my film. Even though I knew I was being unreasonable, I exploded into a fit of rage. I screamed. I slammed my fist on the countertop and stomped my feet. The owner and the technician didn't understand English well enough to catch everything I said, but they got the point. They stood huddled in the far back of the shop. During a lull in my fit, they offered to give me a new roll of film. I didn't want a new roll of film. I wanted my photos. So I screamed and pounded my fists a bit more. Finally, I calmed down. I left and walked across the street to an Indian restaurant for a sweet *lassi*, a flavored yogurt drink, and some vegetable samosas. Feeling better, I signed up for a massage at my hotel. Thai massages are akin to a wrestling smack-down; the masseur is the wrestler, and the cot is the ring. My masseur pulled, chopped, and kneaded away eight months of tangled-up knots, plus all the stress from the photo-lab incident. I was still disappointed about my pictures, but my body was too limp to sustain the anger.

Photographs from studios in Chiang Mai, where many Northern Thai go to dress up in styles reminiscent of the Lanna kingdom.

Vietnam

In a mountain village in northern Vietnam, with the Chinese countryside
in the distance, four women wearing candy-apple red and white floral print turbans walked up to me with determined strides
and tugged at my braids. As I stood there, they both groped my tresses from the hairline to the ends. One even put a braid up to
her nose and smelled it. A little later, a woman with a mound of red and black yarn spiraled around her head as wide as a tire
came over and stabbed me in the arm with her finger. She pinched a section of flesh, pulled up an inch of skin, and released
it—as if to see if it was attached. Then she raised my sleeve up to my shoulders to see if the brown continued all the way up.

They were *montagnards,* a French label for "mountain people." They naturally reminded me of the Chao Khao in Thailand, and of the people I'd expected to see in China. But their unique costumes made it clear that they belonged to distinctive cultures all their own. The women with the floral turbans were Red Dzao, a subgroup of the Dzao montagnards. Their
turbans were tall with rounded, smooth sides and crisp folds at the bottom. The woman with the spiral of yarn around her
head was Red Hmong. Two foot-long strands of black and red yarn were swooped over and under each other creating a
uniquely bloated headdress. We were all in an outdoor market along a narrow road that led to a larger market in Muong
Hum, higher up in the mountains. My stay in Vietnam included visits with montagnards in three communities: Muong
Hum, Sapa, and the outdoor market between the two.

Previous spread (left to right): A Ha Nhi woman in the market in Muong Hum wraps her thick braid of black yarn over a thin headband; Young Red Dzao girls in the square in Sapa; a Black Hmong child in the hills near Sapa.

This page: The *montagnards* often combine materials to create unique headdresses. Right: A Red Hmong woman and child in Muong Hum. Below: A Red Dzao in her red headwrap with colorful tassels. Bottom: A Red Hmong girl in a black and white-checked, beaded turban.

The Dzao and the Hmong are two of Vietnam's fifty-four ethnic groups. The largest group is the Kinh, or indigenous Vietnamese. The other fifty-three are separate minority nationalities that immigrated to Vietnam from Burma, Laos, Cambodia, and China. The Vietnamese call the ethnic groups in the north *dong bao thuong,* which roughly translates as "fellow highland countrymen." Within one group are many subgroups that share general characteristics such as language, culture, and architecture. Within each subgroup, different village communities have their own distinctive costumes and rituals. Among the Dzao alone, there are Dzao Quan Trang ("Dzao with white trousers"), Dzao Quan Chet ("Dzao with tight trousers"), Dzao Tien ("Dzao with coins"), Dzao Thanh Y ("Dzao with blue dresses"), Dzao Do ("Red Dzao"), and at least fourteen other variations.

Back in Sapa, and up ahead in Muong Hum, the ethnic subgroups were completely different, and so were the headwraps. In the hills surrounding Sapa, the Black Hmong wear two- to four-inch-high pillbox-type turbans made from indigo-dyed cotton. Many families have their own dyeing and weaving facilities under the bases of

Left: A Red Hmong woman at a roadside market between Sapa and Muong Hum. Her impromptu headdress is lighter and provides more shade than her traditional red and black turban. Top: A Black Hmong woman in Sapa. Above: A Ha Nhi man in Muong Hum.

their stilt houses, and young girls sit in the countryside with their friends and cross-stitch geometric designs for their clothes.

The local Red Dzao wear solid red headscarves trimmed with white borders or decorated with red puffs of yarn. Red Dzao girls form their small squares of fabric into single-layer head ties with a knot in the front. Adults make large headdresses, tying the fabric around their heads so that it cascades down over their shoulders.

Above: Two Red Dzao (left and center) and a Flower Hmong woman (right) from in and around Sapa. Below: A Red Dzao woman.

Wearing the only store-bought headscarves in Sapa are the Flower Hmong, who wear plaid scarves with bright green, yellow, red, and hot pink lines and loose thread along the fringe. I saw the same plaid scarves further north in Muong Hum, where the Sunday market is set up on a gravel lot in the center of rolling green and brown mountain slopes. The market has four rows of vendors, two on the edges and two that share a center platform and tent. Most vendors were Ha Nhi women, who wear large braids of hair and yarn wound in one large circle around their heads. Others were Red Dzao, with large red and yellow tassels along the edges of their headdresses, and Red Hmong, with their spirals of loose yarn. Among them, they sold loose yarn, sugarcane, fabric, fruit, and vegetables. Circulating about were Black Hmong men, who wear tightly wound black and indigo cotton turbans with thick squares of embroidery and beadwork poking out from the centers.

Most of the men sat in groups, balancing on their haunches and smoking cigarettes or large bamboo bongs. When people sit on their haunches, their bottoms are tucked close to their heels and nearly touch the ground. I'd marveled at the balancing act in other countries. I had noticed men as old as eighty and children as young as two sitting this way—and had even tried to do it myself a couple of times, with little success. After eating a bowl of steamed rice in a tin-roofed shack across the street from the market, I decided to look closely at how the men were sitting and try it again in earnest.

Now, there's a fine art to staring at someone when you don't speak their language,

Left: Family portraits were popular in Hanoi in the early 1950s, before most people stopped wearing turbans on a daily basis. Below: Women's turbans, or *khan quans*, were wound toward the back of the head to display the part in the middle of the hair, a sign of feminine virtue, as seen in this portrait from the 1940s.

and then trying to imitate what they're doing. I ran the risk of offending them, which in turn could have led to all sorts of misunderstandings. But the day was warm, the air was thin, and my spirits were high, so why not? I squatted down, angled my legs, arched my back, adjusted my body weight to the balls of my feet, then the heels. I toppled over. I tried it again: stare, squat, angle, arch, adjust. Topple over. I tried it a third time with the same result. I was with two English tourists who joined in, and we enlisted our Vietnamese guide to offer us pointers. The locals laughed at us at first, then graciously demonstrated how the squat was done. Our persistence never quite paid off.

A bride dressed in a traditional *khan quan* for a wedding in Oklahoma.

After three days, I left the montagnards and traveled to Hanoi, where I spent my mornings imitating the tai chi practitioners by Hoan Kiem Lake and my afternoons wandering the city looking for remnants of traditional Vietnamese headdresses. They were hard to find. It's believed that northern Vietnamese women wore turbans until the 1950s. Up until the nineteenth century, the style was to wrap the hair like a sausage inside of a strip of cotton or velvet, then wind the roll around the head, leaving a tuft of hair protruding from the side. The result was called a *duoi ga*, or "rooster tail," and it sat far enough from the hairline so that a few inches of hair showed in the front. (The front portion of the hair was separated with a part down the middle, which represented a woman's moral and feminine virtues.) In the 1800s, northern men began wearing turban-shaped hats known as *khan xeps*. Northern women switched to turbans, or *khan quans,* which—with the middle part still showing in the front—neatly positioned a narrow strip of fabric into a wide, tightly wound circle toward the back of the head. Urban women usually used black velvet, and rural women used dark brown cotton. Southern Vietnamese women generally kept their hair pulled back into a chignon, or bun.

In the nineteenth century, after the French conquest of Vietnam, young urban women abandoned their turbans and became the first generation of Vietnamese women to fully expose their hair. In rural areas, many women continued to wear traditional dress, which became a symbol of their silent opposition to French colonialism. By the 1940s, the turbans had almost completely disappeared, and other elements of Vietnamese national dress were abandoned in the 1960s. Today, khan quans sometimes surface for weddings, traditional festivals, and family portraits. They tend to be worn in blue, red, pink, and white fabrics. Many older women in Hanoi still consider the traditional khan quans to be proper dress attire, and some even wear a simple version of them when doing their morning tai chi by the lake.

In Vietnam men's hats are designed to look like turbans.

"Many people consider the *non* to be the national headgear of Vietnam," said an older woman who sat on a bench along Hoan Kiem Lake, speaking of the wide, angled bamboo hats worn throughout the country. "The non is fine, and I have one. But I don't wear it very often. I prefer my khan quan," she said.

"Most people today don't wear either," said Vu Van Yen, editor in chief of Vietnam Airways *Heritage* magazine. My trip coincided with the April–May 2001 issue, which included an article on modern women's hairstyles in Vietnam. "Women today like to style their hair, and many young women and tourists don't know how much the style has changed," she said. Before I read the article, I was among the clueless. I asked her during an interview in Hanoi if she'd gotten any feedback on the article. "Oh, yes," she said. "People always want to know about the past, but how else can they learn if nobody writes about it?"

Malaysia

There are baths, and then there are bucket baths. For nine months, the simple luxury of a hot bath in a real tub eluded me, while cold showers and bucket baths became all too familiar. For the uninitiated, a bucket bath involves carrying pots of scalding hot water into the bathroom and then emptying them into a two- or five-gallon plastic bucket. Nearby is a small plastic pail. The key to a good bucket bath is making proper use of the pail, which serves as a separate basin for your soap and washcloth. You have to dip the pail into the bucket, then dip your towel and soap into the pail. The dirty water from the pail is poured down the drain, and the bucket water is kept clean for the next person. All of this has to be done very quickly, as the bucket of hot water is for everyone in the household to share. More important, without the constant stream of warm water from a showerhead, most of the body is always cold and left as an open target for mosquitoes.

I thought about those days while taking the first hot bubble bath of my trip. I was in a hotel in Melaka, a port city in southern Malaysia. After walking away from an affordable, but truly disgusting, hotel room—chipped paint, rusty shower, stained sheets—I stumbled onto a four-star hotel that had temporarily reduced its rates to something even I could manage. My room turned out to be incredible—big, clean, well-appointed. I quickly ran to the supermarket next door and bought bubble bath, nail polish, a nail file, and fresh grapes. When I returned, I was torn between relaxing in my new mini-spa and leaving to search the city for headwraps. With a wistful look at my tub, I decided to get started while I still had some daylight.

Melaka turned out to be a great starting point for Malaysian headdresses. Since 1396, when the city was founded, the rulers and male nobility of Melaka had worn versions of the very turbans that Malaysia's heads of state wear today. Paintings in the city's Cultural Museum depict Parameswara, the prince from Sumatra who founded the port city, wearing a *tengkolok*, or turban. In the paintings, Parameswara's tengkolok is a narrow length of twisted fabric tied like a headband, with a small corner protruding upward through the layers on one side and a jewel pinned to the front. Because he was the sultan, Parameswara's tengkolok is painted yellow, the traditional color of royalty among the Malay. His guards and the men in his court are shown with red, green, and purple tengkoloks.

In 1957, when Malaysia became a country of federated states, the nine states with royal families continued their tradition of wearing tengkoloks. The modern turbans are made with narrow strips of *sogket*, a stiff fabric woven with gold thread. The width and height of each king's headdress vary slightly. In the front, each turn of the layers is raised incrementally so that the turban has an angled incline above the forehead. Instead of a jewel, each king has his state crest pinned to the front. The *agong*, or supreme ruler of Malaysia, wears a *tengkolok diraja*, or royal headwrap, in yellow sogket with the crest of Malaysia pinned to the front. Tengkoloks are generally worn at official state ceremonies and replaced by *songkoks*, or caps, at other times.

Tengkoloks are also worn by grooms on their wedding day. In honor of a custom dating back to the days of Parameswara, in which a common man who's about to be married is *raja se-hari*, or "king for a day," grooms are dressed and pampered like royalty. In the 1300s, male farmers and laborers were restricted to wearing *sampings*— plain turbans made from inexpensive cloth. But on their wedding day, they were allowed to put on tengkoloks, often for the first and only time in their lives.

Today, ready-made tengkoloks are sold in bridal boutiques similar to one I visited in Melaka. At Justina's bridal shop on the western edge of town, the store window had male mannequins dressed in bright blue, lavender, and canary yellow tengkoloks with two-inch decorative brooches above their foreheads. Inside, a display case was filled with similar headdresses, all preshaped and stitched in varying styles and fabrics. Those interested in learning how to tie their own tengkoloks some-

Previous spread (left to right): An Iban man from Sarawak dances the "Ngajat" or warrior dance; Iban and Bidayuh men from Sarawak during a festival; Malay woman draped with a patterned scarf.

Left: In Kuala Lumpur, a typical Malay wedding, called a *bersanding*.
Above: A groom in Sabah wearing a traditional *tanjak*.
Below: Gold headpieces, or *cucuk sangguls*, are often worn in lieu of head scarves at some Malay ceremonies.

times attend workshops like the one at the Pasir Salak Cultural Centre in the north-western state of Perak.

On the island of Borneo, indigenous peoples of Sabah and Sarawak developed their own turbans, calling them *tanjaks*, *sigars*, *sundis*, and other names, depending on the ethnic group. The way the men's turbans are wound is similar to the way the tengkoloks are constructed. Sabah men use squares of colorful, handwoven cloth known as *kain dastars*, which is thicker than sogket and produces bulkier, more varied turbans. Styles range from traditional headbands of folded fabric to more modern and creative turbans with wide folds and curves. They are mostly worn at weddings and traditional ceremonies. When traditional styles are called for, young men often rely on the expertise of village elders.

Ceremonial headgear among Malaysian women depends primarily on their ethnic group and includes decorative hats, gold headpieces known as *cucuk sangguls,* beads, and combs. Women in Negeri Sembilan just north of Melaka, however, wear headwraps made from ceremonial textiles that are folded into broad inverted pyramids. The style comes from Sumatra, the same island that Parameswara was from. In the days of the Melaka sultanate, Minangkabau people from western Sumatra immigrated to the Malay peninsula. The inverted pyramid of the Negeri Sembilan women is a version of the many headdresses still worn by Minangkabau women on Sumatra.

Muslim Malay women are known for their silk, cotton, or batik hijabs, known as *tudungs* in Bahasa Malaysian, the local language. The style was widespread by the 1700s, then faded away in some regions in the 1800s, just as men's sampings, tengkoloks, and kain dastars disappeared from everyday use. Tudungs experienced a brief revival in the 1970s after the Iranian revolution sparked widespread Islamic awakening. "It became fashionable to wear tudungs," recalled a businesswoman traveling from Kuala Lumpur. "People that were Muslim wanted to show that they were proud of Islam." By the 1990s, many Muslim women again put aside their tudungs. Then, in 2000, the women's wing of the Pan-Malaysian Islamic Party ruled that Muslim women employed by the government would be required to cover their heads.

"We don't have to wear headscarves to prove we are Muslim," said a Malay shop

Above: A woman from Negeri Sembilan wears a ceremonial headdress.
Right: Bidayuh men and women perform a traditional dance.

owner who invited me to her home. The woman living next door to her disagreed. "A woman cannot say she is Muslim and then not follow the instructions of the Prophet," she explained. In the basement of the neighbor's home, children were learning from the Qur'an. "My husband gives lessons every day," she said. Sitting apart from the boys in the class was a little girl in a dark purple tudung. My presence distracted her from her studies, and she looked up at me. Not wanting to get her into trouble, I quickly left.

As had become my habit over the previous three days, I returned to my hotel room like a guided missile, where I threw down my notes and focused on one of the few indulgences of my travels. I soaked in a deep porcelain tub of bubbles and hot water. More bucket baths awaited me in the Philippines, and cold showers were still to come in Trinidad. But for one week in Malaysia, everything was just right.

Muslim girls often begin wearing *tudungs* when they are five or six.

The Philippines

In the sixteenth-century epic *Darangen*, passed on orally for centuries among the Maranao people of Mindanao, a frightened mother packs a colorful suit of clothes for her son before he leaves on a dangerous mission, hoping that the power harnessed within the color will protect him like armor. Also in *Darangen*, when the hero prince wears a magnificently colored turban to visit the sultan's daughters, the women are powerless against the prince's charm and the splendor of his headgear.

There are a number of similar centuries-old stories from many of the tribes in the southern Philippines that describe the power of color and its ability—through clothing such as shoulder cloths, waistbands, and turbans—to confer protection and strength on warriors and heroes. This belief in the power of color inspired people to create elaborately woven, beaded, and embroidered textiles with bright yellow, green, pink, red, orange, blue, and black designs, shapes, and patterns. Many of the designs accentuate artistically wrapped turbans. For instance, in an illustration from 1848, a Malay chief on Jolo Island wears a head cloth with a thin, light-colored border that emphasizes the unique draping of the turban.

From at least the second century, most villages in the southern Philippines developed their own turban textiles. The Tausug people on Jolo Island created a patterned head cloth, or *pis;* the Yakan people on Basilan Island created a square head cloth, or *seputangan;* the Subanen people in western Mindanao designed *tulapuks, mansalas,* and *terongs.* Some head

Previous spread: These images are all
from the early 1900s. Left to right:
Subanen man in Sindangan Bay,
Mindano; Ifugao men from Luzon
Island perform a traditional dance;
a Kalinga woman.
This page, right: Bagabo men in Davao,
Mindanao. Below: Batak women near
the Babuyan River.
Opposite page: Tinguianes men in
northwest Luzon (above) and an Ifugao
warrior in traditional hero's headdress
(below).

ties were simple. In a photo from 1910, now at the Field Museum in Chicago, a Bukidnon warrior from north-central Mindanao is dressed in a protective suit of padded abaca cloth and a turban made from an unadorned square of cloth. It is secured on his head from back to front with the ends doubled around and tied in a single knot above the forehead. In other photos at the Field Museum, all Bukidnon men are shown wearing headwraps of some kind, with boys wearing rounded, tubular turbans.

In other tribes and among men of different status, headwraps were more elaborate. In an early twentieth-century photo of a Maranao royal family, the sultan

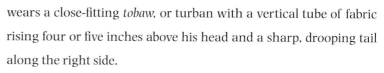

wears a close-fitting *tobaw*, or turban with a vertical tube of fabric rising four or five inches above his head and a sharp, drooping tail along the right side.

There are dozens of other headwraps and head ties—some traditional, some modern—throughout the southern Philippines. To see them and to investigate their origins, I'd planned to spend two

weeks on the islands of Mindanao, Sulu, and Jolo. But as soon as I arrived in Manila, my plans were changed. Mindanao, Sulu, and Jolo are fiercely Islamic strongholds with a violent history of clashes with the predominantly Christian government. My host family and a counselor at the U.S. Embassy insisted that if I traveled to the south, I would risk being kidnapped, raped, and even beheaded. They recited numerous recent abductions and tortures by tribal militant groups. In one month alone—from March 20 to April 23, 2000—thirty-three Filipinos and nineteen foreigners had been abducted. A Catholic priest was beheaded a year before that during a rescue operation, and some of the children and teachers captured with the priest were reportedly raped and killed. "Fundamentalist groups have taken so many people that it's dangerous to step foot on their islands without a military escort," said the counselor. I was crushed.

If the decision to not go was hard, deciding where to go instead was even harder. I tried going north to Banaue, a small town of Ifugao people 340 miles north of Manila. Since before the Spanish arrived in the sixteenth century, Ifugao warriors

This Ifugao woman from Banaue wears a traditional warrior headdress, which she uses as a ploy to get donations from tourists in exchange for photos.

had worn horned and feathered ceremonial headdresses, and I figured I'd search for signs that they also wore turbans. Most didn't. I spent a few days in Banaue, home to a breathtaking landscape of 2,000-year-old irrigated rice terraces cultivated along the town's fertile mountain slopes. Traveling north past Bontok are small rivers and streams, scattered rice terraces, and small towns. There, Kalinga men, often referred to as "the peacocks of the north" because of their bright feather headdresses, use old textiles to cover their heads during rituals. "The textiles are very, very old—with holes throughout," explained a European curator of Filipino art and textiles. "They believe that spirits enter the textiles through the holes." As for traditional headdresses, most ethnic groups in the region prefer to use feathers, wood, boar's tusks, flowers, and shells for ceremonial headpieces, and nothing at all for everyday wear. The few men who wear head ties wear simple, unadorned strips of cloth, usually to help protect them from the cold. A photograph of a Sagada man by Eduardo Masferre that hangs in the Bontok museum north of Banaue shows this style. Frank Longid, a Filipino producer of film documentaries, told me these turbans were also used as "pockets" in which to "stuff cigarettes and such."

Determined to see the colorful, traditional turbans that I'd come for—yet still come out alive—I carefully chose an ethnic group on Mindanao that had kept away from the violence. I made my way to the tranquil banks of Lake Sebu in the south-central part of the island. There, I spent a few days with the T'boli. The biggest things I had to worry about were mosquitoes in the bathroom and a colony of pinhead-sized creatures in my bed.

The T'boli's turbans were as colorful as I'd imagined head cloths would be in that part of the country. Men's turbans, which are rarely worn today, are bright squares of cotton cloth similar to madras. They are woven with one- to two-inch red squares divided by bold yellow, green, and black lines. "Our turbans used to be made from abaca cloth," explained the owner of the T'boli Cultural Museum. The fibers from abaca trees are still harvested, washed, dried in the sun, and woven into textiles, but not for head cloths. For those, the T'boli switched to imported cotton and synthetic fabrics in the 1960s when Maguindanao traders from the Maranao region began making inroads. "This is softer and easier to wash," she said, holding up the bright cloth. To demonstrate how the turbans are tied, the woman asked a man from across the gravel road to put one on. Like most T'boli men today, he only wears the head tie for traditional occasions. "You should come back during a festival," he said. The turban was surprisingly simple. It had a single knot to the side, and the single fold at the top was arranged so that each end spread out at an angle over his ears. With it, he put on one of the traditional jackets, which are still made of abaca cloth.

Women's ceremonial headgear consists of an umbrella-style sun hat, or *s'laong kenibang*, with a bright red, appliquéd cloth draped on top. The cloth is decorated with beads and has beaded fringes hanging from the ends. With the exception of a few women sitting on their front porches, who wore small head ties and loosely wound head coverings made from Maguindanao cloth, no one else around the lake wore headdresses. It seemed as if my quest for headwraps in the Philippines had come to an end. Tempted to break the promises I'd made to the counselor at the embassy and to the family I'd stayed with in Manila, I thought about scouting around for more ethnic groups. "You don't want to do that, Miss," said a young boy who'd helped me find my way to Lake Sebu and came to my hotel for a visit before I left. "The things they say are true. You don't belong here, and something bad could happen." Disappointed, I headed back to Manila and left the country ahead of schedule to go to Indonesia.

A Bontok man from northern Luzon (top) and a T'boli from Lake Sebu, Mindanao (bottom).

Indonesia

I celebrated my birthday while in Indonesia by eating fried sweet-potato cakes on the banks of Lake Singkarak in West Sumatra. The lake was more like a small gulf—almost ten miles wide and surrounded by a vast range of tree-covered mountains. My sweets were local favorites—crispy, orange mounds of deep fried, tooth-decaying sugar and starch. I'd bought them off the cooling racks of a small dessert factory that also grinds local coffee beans and sells bananas dipped in tapioca flour and deep fried. Sitting by the lake was a break in my tour of the Minangkabau heartland, where the Minangkabau people have dozens of unique ceremonial and everyday headdresses.

Known as *tangkuluaks*, Minangkabau headwraps range from elaborate constructions of height, width, and style to simple coverings that drape loosely over the head in a collection of styles dictated by ideology, tradition, status, geography, and—in the case of ceremonial headdresses—the role the wearer will play in the ceremony. Some women's ceremonial headdresses rise upward at an incline double the height of a woman's head and slope down to the nape of the neck. Others are bisected down the middle and have rolled or angled horns that protrude on either side. Most are made from shoulder cloths known as *salendangs*, which are skillfully woven with gold thread and symbolic motifs.

As early as the thirteenth century, mothers began weaving salendangs for their daughters' dowries when the children were only five years old. In today's prices, it takes as much as $200 and two months of working every day to weave a salen-

A *salendang* headdress from Payakum-buh. Page 161, left: Minangkabau women at a Baptism dinner. The woman in the black headdress wears a traditional *tangkuluak*, while the other women wear more modern styles. Right: A conservative *tangkuluak* worn with a decorative brooch to pull the fabric tight around the face.
This page: The complicated *salendang* headdress of Sungayang village (top) and the less fussy, but popular, cotton and lace ceremonial *tanduk* (bottom).

dang that's only one meter long. The gold thread is imported from China and India. The loom and the black thread come from local towns, such as Silungkang, Minangkabau's center of weaving. Today, few women know how to work the complicated looms or have the time and money necessary to make salendangs. "We don't wear them very often," explained an employee at the dessert factory. "There are fewer and fewer ceremonies today. We work during the week, so the only time for ceremonies is on the weekend." At the ceremony, everyone isn't obligated to wear a salendang headdress either. If it's a wedding, of course the bride wears one, and maybe her mother. "For most people, salendangs are too expensive to buy, so we rent one if we need it," she said.

At the Aladdin Art and Antique Shop in Bukittinggi, many salendangs cost $400 or more. Mr. H. A. Sutan Madjo Indo, the owner, keeps them rolled up on shelves behind the cash register. Hanging on a wall near the salendangs is a photograph of his daughter wearing a ceremonial headdress. Mr. Indo and his wife unrolled the salendangs for me, stressing the importance of keeping them away from sunlight, never folding them, and never washing or dry cleaning them. They pointed out the various motifs that were woven into the textiles, such as pineapples, trees, and fish, and explained how the motifs and the weave vary from village to village. "Women rarely wear salendangs from other villages, and we never wear salendangs made by other ethnic groups," explained Mrs. Indo. The center of each salendang was thinly woven with black silk or cotton thread, and the ends were stiff with heavy concentrations of gold thread. Hanging from the ends were the loose threads, cut from the loom and left as decoration.

A few miles from Bukittinggi, in a replica of the thirteenth-century Minangkabau kingdom palace that burned in the 1970s, a young college student was about to put on a salendang headdress for the first time. Her name was Rika, and she was spending the day with her grandmother, who was originally from Minangkabau but had moved to Java after she got married. A photographer with a trunk load of traditional Minangkabau dress had enticed Rika into having him take a picture, which she agreed to do as a gift to her grandmother. Rika selected a long, black dress with gold embroidery and a bright yellow and black headdress engineered into two large, upside-down cones, angled upward on each side of the headdress. The prewrapped and sewn headdress was slightly too small for her head. "It's not exactly right, and it's not the style of my people, but it's very beautiful. My grandmother wants to see me in it, so I'm happy to do this for her," said Rika. Her grandmother watched from the palace steps, where she sat in a brown dress and a white *jilbab*, Indonesia's unique version of the hijab. It was unlike any Islamic head covering I'd seen. It had two strings in the front that were pulled back behind her temples and tied into a knot in the back over the fabric. The sides covered her shoulders and were gathered in the front and secured with a large, floral-shaped brooch, so that her entire face was framed with fabric and all of her hair was covered.

Jilbabs were almost unheard of before the 1980s. "Minangkabau women covered their heads with salendangs or tangkuluaks for centuries before Islam came. In other parts of Indonesia, women never used to cover, not even Muslims. When they went to mosques to pray, they draped salendangs over their hair. That was it," explained a man who works in Indonesia's ambassador corps. In an effort to encourage women to wear more typical Islamic head coverings on a regular basis, designers created the jilbab. "Young women don't want to look like old ladies," explained a woman who also works for the ambassador corps. "We didn't have this when I was growing up. Indonesia is 80 percent Muslim. Women didn't wear head coverings. So Muslim designers began experimenting with styles, colors, and materials. The jilbabs are very expensive, you know, because they're made by designers. But they are also very fashionable. A lot of Muslim women wear them all the time now," she said. While in Sumatra, I also saw women both young and old wearing hijabs more typical of other parts of the world—made from attractive squares of fabric and tied at the corners or secured with a brooch.

In the town of Pandai Sikek, an old woman with chiseled cheeks and a beautiful headwrap caught my eye. She was keeping company with the owner of a one-room souvenir shop. Her white cotton tangkuluak with decorative lace trim was spread out around her face like a daisy. It had swooping horizontal folds around the crown of her head, was flared out around the back, and had a pleated tail hanging loose over her left ear. She didn't speak English, so I pulled out a drawing of the same headwrap and used hand gestures to convey how much I liked hers. She smiled and nodded, more at me than with me. When I first held out my camera, she

In the market in Bukittingi, a buyer in a modern *tangkuluak* (top), and merchant in a traditional, non-ceremonial *tanduk* (bottom).

Above: My rare spotting: a man in a *tanduk*.
Below: Three chieftains wearing *detas*.

didn't seem to mind, but as soon as I lifted it up, she shrieked, threw her hands up over her face, and darted out the store, up the hill, and behind a house so fast I didn't have time to stop her and apologize.

Still later, my guide drove past a man sitting on his haunches and smoking a cigarette. He was the first man I'd seen in Indonesia wearing a turban, although since the second century, Indonesian men—from Toraja chiefs in Sulawesi and eastern Sumatra to Javanese warriors on Java—have worn some form of headwrap. Usually made from thin squares of cloth, many are decorated with embroidery, appliqué, or shellwork. Others are made with complicated folds.

The man on the side of the road wore a plaid cotton headwrap with squares of brown, yellow, and gray. It was pulled tight around the left side of his head, knotted on the right side, and fanned out at the end so that it looked like a lollipop.

Still shaken by my experience with the lady in the shop, I was nervous about how he would respond to a request for a photograph. I asked my guide to stop the jeep, and then I coached him on what to say to the stranger. To my surprise, the man couldn't have cared less. He took another puff on his cigarette, blew out the smoke, then gave his okay with a short shrug of his shoulders.

Most men's turbans among the Minangkabau are either *detas* or *saluaks.* Detas are pointed headdresses made from square pieces of cloth. I spotted a version in a portrait in the palace that I visited in Pagaruyung. A prince wore an imposing turban with smooth, rounded sides, an angled peak above the forehead, and a jeweled brooch pinned to the front. It was exactly the same style as the tengkoloks in Malaysia. Today, detas are worn by dancers, musicians, some chieftains, and guards. Saluaks are flat-topped turbans with rounded corners that are folded from a one-meter-long, rectangular piece of batik, silk, or cotton. They are shaped differently from village to village but generally have sharp, horizontal folds in the front that signify the steps leading to the local meeting house, where many ceremonies take place. Different shapes mean different things. A turban that is flat across the top usually signifies the importance of treating everyone equally. A rounded turban signifies a chieftain's calming behavior toward his people.

In the Minangkabau kingdom, men don't start wearing turbans until they are married, and even then, unless they are chiefs, guards, musicians, or dancers, most men wear them only on their wedding day. "If you're married, it's not wrong to wear a turban. It's just that most men don't do it," explained my translator.

While I had him around, I asked him to tell me the secret behind *nasi goreng*, or Indonesian fried rice. Rice had been my staple food in Asia, and my palate delightedly adjusted to each country's version. Indonesia's fried rice is spicy and has more scrambled eggs in it than the versions I'd tried in other countries. There was also something else I couldn't figure out—something that made it my favorite. "Maybe it's the sauce. You know, we use a special paste with tomatoes and spices," he said. "Hmmm," I wondered.

Grateful that I'd lived to see another birthday, I celebrated throughout my week in Indonesia, taking a moment each evening—usually after a plate of nasi goreng—to pray and reflect. As of yet, I hadn't been sick, gotten into any (real) trouble, or faced any problems I couldn't handle. With only a few countries left on my itinerary, I smiled at my good fortune and prepared for the Caribbean.

Solok chiefs wearing traditional *saluaks*.

The Americas
and
The Caribbean

Jamaica

In the middle of Ras Wittie's soliloquy on how mankind would eventually be one race, I got stung by a wasp. Not wanting to interrupt, I quietly tried to suppress the pain by gripping my arm where the stinger had penetrated. Junie, one of the "brethren" sitting next to me in the back seat of the car, noticed my discomfort and asked what was wrong. I told him and he told the other two: Wittie, who was driving, and Milton, an American Christian-turned-Rastafarian who was in Jamaica on pilgrimage. Wittie immediately wanted to take me to a hospital, not because that's what he would have done for himself, but because he wanted to take care of me like the "princess" and *dawtah* he'd accepted me as since we'd first met the afternoon before. Both are terms showing respect for women in the Rastafarian "community." (I sometimes called him "Ras," a common title for Rastafarian men.)

Unfortunately, a hospital was out of the question. We were two hours from Montego Bay on a rural highway near the town of Manderville. We were going to a *binghi*, a celebration and reunion of Nyabinghi Rastafarians, and we were already late. Junie and Milton came up with another idea. Junie took a large pinch of herb, or marijuana, from a plastic sandwich bag and rolled a *spliff*, or cigarette. As he lit it and began smoking, he told me to try and relax, and that he was going to take care of me. By this point, the pain was unbearable. I started digging my nails into his thigh, the seat, my head, and anything else I could grab. Halfway through the spliff, Junie stopped smoking, put out the fire, and unrolled the

cigarette. He let the herb fall into his left hand, added some spit, and mixed the two into a paste. He then pressed the paste into the pain, and within seconds, my anguish had died down. By the time we reached the binghi, the discomfort was completely gone.

At the binghi, I joined in with the spiritual chants, kept warm by the large Judgment Fire, and—late at night—retired to an elevated wood platform in the dawtahs' tent with twenty or so other women and their children.

There were few turbans among the men, who prefer to wear *tams* (knitted or leather caps) if they wear a head covering at all. Nyabinghi women, however, always wear head coverings, which vary between knit caps and headwraps. In the dawtahs' tent, some of us talked for an hour in soft whispers to keep from waking the children. Women explained that "when you see a Rasta princess or dawtah, you know she's a Rasta because of the way she dresses." "We choose to be natural and modest. We don't wear makeup or short dresses, and we cover our hair." This is in part to show their respect for God, or Jah, and for their

Page 168: A Bobo Shanti woman places her hand on her chest as a sign of welcome, inviting me into the compound on Bobo Hill (page 169, left).
Page 169: A Bobo shanti empress near Kingston (center) and a priest in western Jamaica (right).
This page: A Bobo Shanti man dressed in his version of a turban worn by Haile Selassie. Opposite page: Itah, a Nyabinghi Rastafarian, in one of her daily creations.

husbands. Also, women's headwraps, they explained, "hide the power of self" that's embedded in their locks. They believe that a woman's essence is concentrated in her hair, and "that essence—our beauty—should not be revealed to anyone but our husbands. That is why we cover our hair."

Back in Montego Bay, where many Nyabinghis live, I met Anita, who said that she never goes outside without her head covered. "My husband is good, and would respect my decision if I ever chose not to wear a headwrap, but I don't choose to. I respect him and our union. When I'm at home, my wrap and all of my defenses come off. That's when my husband sees all of me—my soul, my spirit, and my beauty. Why should anyone else see that?" she said.

There's no specific style, although most women maintain that their headwraps, like their clothes, should be modest. A brassy exception was Itah, a spirited woman in her late forties who wore Montego Bay's most eye-catching headwraps. She creates a different style every day by incorporating her long locks into the turban design, then accessorizing it with gold chains, cowrie shells, and beads. I met her as she was giving a donation to a Rastafarian street vendor in Sam Sharpe Square in downtown Montego Bay. She'd assembled a dramatic turban by wrapping bright solid yellow fabric tightly around her hairline and over a vertical loop of braided locks. Another day, she created a brilliant white headwrap that was tall and narrow, with shells and beads wrapped around it. "Headwraps are my personal expressions," she said.

Nyabinghis are one of three main Rastafarian groups in Jamaica. Among the Bobo Shanti Rastafarians near Kingston, eye-catching headwraps are discouraged—perhaps even forbidden. The Bobo Shanti are the most orthodox of the Rastafarian groups. Although they share the same core beliefs as the Nyabinghi (that Haile Selassie, the former emperor of Ethiopia, was divine; that Jah is within everyone; and that Marcus Garvey was a prophet), the Bobo Shanti are as different from the Nyabinghi as Baptists are from Methodists. One of their most visible differences is in how they cover their hair.

A sprawling Bobo Shanti commune is located on Bobo Hill—also known as City on the Hill, a mountaintop several miles west of Kingston. A thin man with a goatee and a tightly wrapped, apple-red turban that slanted upward into a blunt point had seen my car approach. He met me a few yards down the hill from the commune and escorted me to the ten-foot-tall green, yellow, and red picket fence that lined the perimeter of the compound. Before entering, I was interviewed by a priest (Bobo Shanti men are either priests or prophets) in a blue turban, also shaped into a tight, tubular wrap, and then by a woman in a simple headscarf, who was holding a large calendar. After some very kind pleasantries, she came to the point: When had I last menstruated? The man before her had hinted around the subject but obviously

Inside the Bobo Shanti compound, all women and children keep their hair completely covered.

thought the matter was best discussed between two women. She held up the calendar and explained that a menstruating woman, or a woman who has menstruated within the past twenty-one days, could not enter the compound. (This only affects outsiders. Bobo Shanti women, of course, come and go, but they do have to respect certain boundaries.) That left me a window of nine or ten days, which, fortunately, was sufficient.

Having settled that, I still couldn't enter until I redid my headwrap. I'd tied a modest, compact turban on my head, which was acceptable in Nyabinghi circles. For the Bobo Shanti, however, I had to take it off, fold it into a triangle, and drape it over my forehead so that the two outside corners could be tied into a knot at the nape of my neck and the rest of the fabric could hang past my shoulders and completely cover my hair. As luck would have it, my piece of cloth wasn't long enough, so the woman went back inside the compound and returned with one of her scarves. She tied it for me, asked me to recite a short prayer, and then invited me in.

Once inside, I was greeted as an empress and a dawtah. I was invited to sit on a bench near a small sentry post and office. Rising up the peak in front of the bench was a beautiful, serenely peaceful garden of flowers and white painted rocks. Small wooden buildings and Rastafarian flags were also in the distance. My hostess sat beside me and began explaining why headscarves are important. "Mary, mother of Jesus, wore a scarf, and so should we. We wear our head ties simply, like Mary did," she said. Stopping to pick up her little girl, who also wore a head tie, she continued. "It's not about fashion and new styles. It's about paying respect to Jah."

Showing respect through one's headdress also extends to Bobo Shanti men, whose turbans symbolize their devotion to Haile Selassie—who wore a turban during his coronation in 1930—and to Jah. "In the Old Testament, priests wore turbans and robes," explained the priest. I was inside the guardhouse at this point. On the wall was a photograph of men chanting in white turbans. "We wear white on the Sabbath," he said, referring to Saturdays, the same day of rest recognized by the Ethiopian Orthodox Church.

Turbans set Bobo Shanti men apart from other Rastafarians, an important distinction since at least the 1950s. The Bobo Shanti culture is a way of life, and a person's headdress is a sign that he or she has accepted that life. Young men studying to join the Bobo Shanti are not automatically given the honor of wearing a turban. "He has to earn the respect of his brethrens and sistrens, and gain the knowledge and wisdom of the Bobo Shanti culture," one man explained.

I stayed in Kingston for only a couple of days, then returned to Montego Bay—or, to be more precise, to the beaches of Montego Bay. When I'd arrived in Jamaica a week earlier, a care package of swimsuits and comfort food had been waiting for me at the guesthouse, courtesy of my sister, Tracy. For the first time in nearly ten months, I was back in the Western Hemisphere and had a canister of Pringles, fresh socks, and a huge smile on my face to prove it. Jamaica was not only in the same time zone as New York, but it was also the first predominantly black country I'd been in since Ethiopia, and the first country since the United Arab Emirates where I didn't need an English translator.

I was surprisingly aware of all of this and felt the need to celebrate, which I did by visiting the gorgeous beaches of Negril and Montego Bay. At night, I went to clubs, and whenever I saw another American I'd introduce myself and catch up on events that hadn't made the world news. Very few Jamaicans outside of the Rastafarians wear headwraps, so when I wasn't with the Nyabinghi or Bobo Shanti, I tried to relax and pamper myself a little. Still, I felt most at home with the Nyabinghi, particularly Anita, who had showed me around and introduced me to her friends. Of course, that meant I had to wear a headwrap and dress modestly when I was with them, but it was worth it just to be surrounded by so many nice people.

Trinidad

So far in my travels, I hadn't once walked the streets or gone to a church dressed improperly. So what was it about Trinidad that made me lose my mind? On one humiliating night I actually showed up at a Spiritual Shouter Baptist church bareheaded and dressed in a slinky, sleeveless mini-dress. I'd just bought the dress the day before, and since I'd seen lots of women in Trinidad wearing shorts and short skirts, I didn't think anything of it. On the day of the fiasco, I'd been in Port of Spain doing research, and before I knew it, it was time to set off for Tunapuna, a small community outside of Port of Spain where the Mount Horeb Spiritual Baptist Church awaited. The trip would involve squeezing into a crowded taxi at the shared car depot near the harbor, transferring to a "maxi-taxi" (mini-van) that got me closer to the church, and then walking the rest of the way. Not wanting to get lost or be late, I was completely focused on everything except for how I was dressed.

I arrived at the church just before sunset with the hem of my thigh-high mini swishing in the wind and my hair bobbing in a ponytail of long braids. I must have looked absolutely disrespectful. Shouter Baptist women don't dress like that, especially not when they're about to worship the Lord. They dress modestly, and before they enter a church they cover their heads with headwraps that hide their hair. Styles vary from simple to fanciful depending on the occasion, the fabric, and individual taste. Wearing a head covering is so important to Shouter Baptist women that many wear them outside of

Page 174: All dressed up in honor of Emancipation Day. Page 175: Two women, a Rastafarian in Port-of-Spain (left) and a Ghanian in San Fernando (right) teach women how to wrap Afrocentric turbans.

This page: A Shouter Baptist woman outside of the Mount Horeb Spiritual Baptist Church in Tunapuna.

church as well. Archbishop Barbara Gray-Burke of the Ark of the Covenant Spiritual Baptist Church, a Shouter Baptist church in Laventille in eastern Trinidad, later told me in a phone interview that most women wear headwraps because they serve as portals for spiritual visitations. "It's important to be prepared," she said. "When I get a visitation from the spirits, what they tell me helps guide me. If my head is uncovered, how can I accept the visitation?" she continued, adding that she gets migraines if she walks outside without her head tie.

For me, the only thing worse than not wearing a head covering was not realizing that I wasn't wearing one. This put the leader—which is what the head of the church is called—and members of his congregation in the awkward position of having to bring it to my attention.

When I arrived at Mount Horeb I discovered a converted garage attached to Leader McDonald Sergeant's house. The church was founded in the late 1940s by his aunt at a time when the Spiritual Shouter Baptist religion was outlawed. Early in the 1900s, the police and British colonial officials had received numerous complaints about the noise Shouter Baptists were making. This led to the Shouters Prohibition Ordinance of 1917, which banned the religion and all typical Shouter Baptist activities, including playing drums, singing, shouting, ringing bells, and even wearing white head ties. The prohibition lasted for thirty-four years, forcing church members to set up secret meeting houses in the hills and in unconventional locations such as shacks, garages, and attics.

Leader Sergeant presided over a single, spotless room of white walls and five or six rows of polished wooden pews separated by a center aisle. A shrine with candles, a vase, and a plant sat on a small, round altar near the front of the church. Against the far wall, an altar with a pyramid of white candles and ivy trim was gated behind a small metal barrier.

Service hadn't started yet, so I was invited inside the leader's home. Beyond the panel-covered living room, with a hat rack in the corner and stuffed animals on an old TV, the leader sat at the kitchen table eating fish cakes. Joining him was Agatha, a member of his congregation. She was wearing a powder-blue and white dress and a matching headwrap. The headwrap was tied close to her head with a twist in the front and the ends tucked underneath in the back. She washed dishes while the pastor talked. He explained that Christian women have always worn headwraps. "In the old days, you never seen women without their head ties," he said. "It's a sign of respect, for themselves, for God and for Jesus Christ." Like the Bobo Shanti in Jamaica, Leader Sergeant drew on the example of the Virgin Mary and said that women "should be careful about how they dress. They should be modest, and always wear a head tie when they enter the Lord's house."

Hip headwraps such as this one are popular among black women through out Trinidad and Tobago.

Members of his congregation began arriving. Before he went into his room to change, I asked if I could get close to the altar and stay for service. He said yes, as long as I covered my head. That's when I finally got a clue. I gasped with embarrassment and quickly apologized. He brushed aside any offense, pointed me toward the hat rack, and told me to pick one. I selected a burgundy beret and struggled to push, stuff, and tuck every braid into it. Agatha then took me outside and introduced me to other members of the congregation—one in a small brown and white headwrap with ripples on the sides, and another with a snug black turban and small gold earrings. We talked by the front door. At first, I assumed it was to keep me company, but then I realized it was to keep me out of the church. They said I needed something to cover my arms before I could enter, and even then, because of my short dress, it would be inappropriate for me to stay. Again I gasped. I was not making a good impression and didn't know what to do.

Shaking her head and leaving me with a dumb look on my face, Agatha went back into the leader's house. She returned with a white bath towel and draped it over my shoulders. Then, she and the others followed me inside. I headed straight for the altar. A framed picture of Christ hung on the wall to its left. And there I stood right in front of it, in a brown, tie-dyed mini-dress, a burgundy beret, a white bath towel, and a pair of leather flip-flop sandals. The church was filling up, and I was a spectacle to the entire congregation. To make matters worse, my bath-shawl kept sliding off when I raised my arms to take pictures. Blasphemy! Agatha called me back outside of the church, secured the towel with a safety pin, and as nicely as she could, suggested I leave after I finished with my photographs.

The next day, I devoted my time to the Orisha, a religious group based on the faith and rituals of the Yoruba people of West Africa. Similar to members of other

An Orisha girl.

Caribbean religions that are also based on Yoruba beliefs, the Orisha consider the head to be the seat of the human soul and believe that it should be properly adorned (in the Yoruba language, *ori* means "head").

For most Orisha, a headwrap is the ultimate adornment. Some women wear headwraps every day, even in the home. Others only wear them during Orisha ceremonies. "I don't want the people I work with to know that I'm Orisha," said an office worker in Port of Spain. "Orisha isn't considered a major religion. Most people are Catholics or Protestants. If they think you worship *orishas* (a multitude of ancestral spirits), they look at you differently," she said.

Whether Orisha women wear their head ties in public or not, most wear them when they go to the *palais,* or shrine. In the palais, however, if a woman believes that an orisha energy has entered her body during prayer, she'll remove her turban to allow the energy to do what it has come for. Once the energy leaves, she quickly puts the headwrap back on her head.

To better understand Orisha culture, I joined a group of children, teenagers, and teachers in a tree-planting project on the sacred ground of Oshun, the patron saint of the Orisha-based private school that sponsored the trip. The organizer of the field trip, and director of the school, was Pat McCloud, an Orisha priestess. Unlike most women, who wear headwraps in the palais but not in public, McCloud does exactly the opposite. "I don't mind wearing headwraps in public. I love them, and for some social occasions, they are wonderful. But I don't wear them when worshiping," she said. Her reasons are clear. "Wearing headwraps is a custom introduced by the Catholic colonizers. Turbans are not a true tradition of the Yoruba," she explained. The first large wave of European Christians and captured West Africans came to Trinidad in the late 1700s when Spain invited French, Irish, English, and German immigrants to settle the island, inadvertently leading to an increase in the island's slave trade.

"Of course, the Yoruba wear turbans, but not during prayer. Not during rituals. You see how even here, women take off their turbans when an orisha manifests itself. So much was lost during slavery because there weren't any elders to refer to," said McCloud. Once transplanted to Trinidad, Orisha evolved as a collection of competing and complementary Yoruba principles from different tribes and incorporated aspects of Catholicism, in which headscarves played an intricate role. "Because of Catholicism, it's understandable that they [the slaves and the first free Africans in Trinidad] incorporated head ties," explained McCloud. "Some Orisha even say Hail Marys and use the name 'Jesus' synonymously when referring to orisha ancestors," she said.

Joining Orisha and Shouter Baptist women in wearing headwraps in Trinidad are a small minority of locally born Rastafarians and Christian Baptist groups. Once a year, however, for at least a day, and up to a whole week, thousands of black Trinidadians dress in traditional West African attire, including headwraps, to celebrate the 1834 Emancipation Act, which freed slaves in Trinidad and Tobago. To get the right look, many women turn to stylists, such as Margaret Blades, Agnes Charles, and Abilah Jaramogi, ordinary women with a gift for tying gorgeous head ties. Every summer, before the Emancipation Day festivities on August 1, these women and others like them give workshops on how to tie headwraps, and they take orders for the turbanly-challenged. "More than 200 people came to my first workshop," boasted Blades, who said she's been giving classes since 1996. "At first, people weren't really interested in anything related to Africa. But in 1996, things changed, and all of a sudden, people wanted to participate."

Rastafarians make up a colorful minority of men and women who wear headwraps everyday

Emancipation Day has been officially recognized as a holiday since 1985. "It got off to a slow start," said a woman with the Emancipation Support Committee, a group founded in 1992 through the joint efforts of separate Afro-Trini organizations in Trinidad and Tobago. "We found out that people really wanted to celebrate the day. There just needed to be a national campaign to say 'Hey, this is a great thing,'" she said. Women in Port of Spain described Emancipation Day celebrations as the second largest festivity, just behind Carnival. "We wear turbans to work and everyone thinks it's really nice," said one woman.

Trinidad was the last country where I would concentrate on religious-based headwraps. It was a shame that I'd introduced myself so poorly at Mount Horeb, but I recovered quickly and wound up having a terrific time. I even got a chance to *go limin'*, or hang out, with a few locals. We went to one or two clubs a night, and we always found our way back to the Savannah, a large park surrounded by poui trees and large homes. On the night before my departure, I stayed out until 5 A.M., barely leaving myself enough time to get a taxi to the airport. And even then, I almost left one of my bags. Yes, there was something about the Caribbean that was making me lose my mind.

Martinique

"I'm already taken," boasted the spice vendor in the large outdoor market in Fort-de-France. She wouldn't give her name, but she was more than willing to talk about her life and the joy she had living it. The fact that she was married was abundantly clear by her colorful madras with three ascending points. "One point means you're available. I haven't worn a madras with one point since I was a teenager," she beamed. "Two points means you're already spoken for, but another man is welcome to try his luck. Three points, like mine, means your heart is taken and can't be swayed. I've been married for more than thirty years, and my heart is still taken," she said.

To be clear, the spice vendor is one of a kind. Most women in Martinique stopped wearing *madrases*—head ties made with madras fabric—in the mid-1900s.

The brightly colored cotton fabric dyed with multiple red, green, blue, orange, and yellow squares takes its name from the eastern port city of Madras (now called Chennai) in southern India. In the late 1700s, it was exported from India to the French Antilles and was quickly adopted by white Creole women for headcloths. It had a distinctive odor, but the material was light and the vibrant color lasted longer than the dyes in other fabrics at the time. By the early 1800s, black Creole women had embraced madras head ties as well. Madras became the most popular fabric in France's western colonies, and it still commands its own sections in fabric stores throughout Martinique.

As a head tie, madrases were incorporated into a unique dress code based on women's wealth, occupation, race, and even complexion. Head coverings in general came in many styles, and each one played its part to categorize and identify the wearer. In the late 1600s, white Creole women typically wore taffeta and satin dresses and fashionable hairstyles. Over the next century, lighter, more breathable fabrics became popular. Not all head ties were made with madras, but when madras headdresses entered the scene, a Martinican named Fréderic Masson wrote that a revolution was taking place: Women's stylish hairdos were being replaced by *"les mouchoirs à la créole"* or Creole head ties. Those first head coverings ranged from large, tubular turbans, to tightly wrapped head ties with a fist-sized knot on one side and a point hanging down the back, to short, rounded turbans with a high front that sloped down in the rear.

Illustrations depicting seventeenth-century slave women doing laundry show them wearing only short, wraparound skirts and simple turbans and head ties. By the 1800s, their head ties had to be constructed in specific ways that enabled the larger community to know what type of slaves they were—field hands, domestic servants, or laundresses—and therefore, whether they were some-

place where they didn't belong. Plantation and field slaves were given squares of plain white, brown, gray, or violet fabric. Many domestic slave women received madras fabric, but they still had to keep their head ties simple, with small knots in the front and a small, conical point in the back. Even simpler head ties, with a rounded back and sides, were worn by women working on the farms. Women who cut sugarcane fixed their head ties in a series of knots in the back so that two ends dropped to the nape of the neck and the other two fell past the shoulders. Laundresses, often called "salted rivers," wrapped a portion of their head ties smoothly above their ears, then arranged the bulk of the fabric so that the ends fell over the ears and shoulders.

Page 180: This happily married woman wears her three-pointed madras head-tie every day.
Page 181, left: Creole women in St. Pierre, circa 1902; right, a *mulatresse* in a fetching *jupe-chemise*.

Domestic slaves called *ti collets* wore small pieces of silk or satin fixed in place with pins.

Black Creole women wore two basic fashions: the *jupe-chemise* (a lace blouse, the *chemise*, and a hoop skirt, the *jupe*), or the *grand-robe*, a full-length, long-sleeved dress. With them, they always wore stylish madras head ties, often with squares of fine white linen placed underneath. They usually draped and knotted decorative foulards, or scarves, around their shoulders, and accessorized themselves with large gold necklaces, brooches, and earrings.

From two types of madras head ties—the madras with its varied points and the *calendée*, a much smaller, tightly folded turban made with stiff, circular pleats and a single, vertical point—sprung a variety of styles and personal touches. Girls who fell in love and moved out on their own adopted madrases with two points to signify their new lives. As relationships blossomed or fell apart, the points on their madrases increased or decreased accordingly. The calendée was altogether different. Worn like a hat, its signature stiffness was achieved by a *calendeuse*, an artisan who spent two to three days carefully applying yellow paint to the fabric before crafting each headpiece. It was often adorned with gold "trembling pins" and brooches.

In Martinique, a beautifully made turban was admired as being "a head well-tied." Some distinctive styles became associated with specific rituals and professions as well as a woman's marital status. A flamboyant style with a vertical fan of pleated fabric was popular among prostitutes. A white muslin *bailer* (similar to a calendée) was worn with black dresses when mourning the death of a family member, and a madras bailer was worn for festive occasions such as weddings and baptisms. Mothers sometimes rolled down the points of their madrases to show they had children. Older women usually wore head ties with no points, or with a single point off to the side. The family nurse, or *da*, wore a pleated head tie that was similar to a calendée, only larger, with a flared-out point

Opposite page: A *mulatresse* wears her hair in coiled braids wrapped in a one-pointed headtie. This page: A *capresse* wears her hair entirely covered in a three-pointed headtie. Both women wear large gold necklaces, madras shoulder scarves, and wrap skirts.

Top: Grand-robe worn with a madras *foulard* and a headtie.
Bottom: Postcard of a young *capresse* wearing a two-pointed madras.

sticking up and sometimes a lot of jewelry all around it. *Matadors,* or women who ran brothels, often wore stylized headpieces with four points, signifying that they loved everyone. The points were sometimes spread out horizontally over the shoulders and down the back and accompanied by bills of Martinican currency.

A woman's complexion required additional consideration. In Martinique, ethnic distinctions were pronounced. White Creoles, or women of pure European (mostly French) descent, were called *bekes,* and black Creoles in general were referred to as *creoles.* Creole women of pure African descent were known as *negresses,* and Creoles of mixed European and African blood were called mulattoes. Of those, women with very dark skin and curly hair were known as *capresses.* Children of mixed African and Indian blood were called *coolies.* (Male Indians and coolies wore turbans similar to the pagris and safas in India.) An informal system laid out which color was best suited for a woman's complexion. A capresse should wear pale yellow. A light-skinned *mulatresse* looked best in rose, blue, or green, depending on her shade. A negresse should wear white, scarlet, or violet. For black Creole women—mixed or not—wearing stylish and sometimes flamboyant costumes was sometimes the best way to get ahead and improve one's station in life. The head ties were only one part of the entire ensemble that helped them to achieve their goals.

In the 1900s, the world changed, and so did Martinique. France had abolished slavery in 1848, and the industries that relied on slaves had to adjust. Around that time, beke women had mostly abandoned head ties for hats and stylish coiffures. Black Creole women continued to wear the traditional clothes, but worried that their style would be absorbed by the newly freed slaves, they gradually developed a new look. In the late 1880s, calendeuses were getting less and less work from black Creoles, but madrases were still very popular. In 1902, Mount Pelée erupted and St. Pierre, the capital and center of Martinican style, was burned to the ground. The capital was moved to Fort-de-France, but the heyday of the headwrap was over. The traditional costume continued to be worn at weddings, baptisms, First Communions, confirmations, and other special occasions. But by the 1940s, it had finally died out. Many women considered the style passé and wanted to wear modern fashions. More important, black people wanted to distance themselves from everything that remained of the slave era.

In the 1980s, madrases and calendées were revived as an important part of

Martinican culture. Today, a scattered number of Martinicans still wear versions of the old turbans at weddings, costume balls, and formal gatherings. Many modern madrases and calendées can be bought ready-to-wear from small boutiques in Fort-de-France. In one such store, I met a young woman shopping for a madras to wear that night. "I know these points mean something, but I'm not sure what," she said in a panic. "Do I want one point, or two? I feel silly. I should know this, but I don't." The salesclerk smiled and pointed to a white card with illustrations of the historic madrases and clear definitions for the different points. The customer breathed a sigh of relief and bought a headwrap with a single point. "Maybe this will be a hint to all of the single men there," she said with a grin.

Martinican culture shares similarities with the eighteenth- and nineteenth-century culture of New Orleans, which was also colonized by the French, and which became home to many immigrants from the Antilles. I wondered how Martinique's fashions differed from New Orleans style. A part of me wanted to fly straight from Fort-de-France to Louisiana, where I thought I could make strong comparisons. Alas, I still had one more country to visit before returning to the States. I knew I wouldn't find any obvious comparisons between the Mayans and the Creoles, but I was looking forward to exploring Guatemala, just the same.

Shoppers in a boutique in Fort-de-France choose among pre-wrapped and stitched madras headties (on the counter) and *calendées* (elevated on stands).

Guatemala

Guatemala City wasn't exactly what I had expected. Maybe I'd done too much partying in the Caribbean, but when I arrived in Guatemala, I didn't sense the raw excitement I'd anticipated in the only Latin American country of my travels. More important, like most cities in Latin America, people in Guatemala City don't wear traditional headwraps.

So I left. I rode north in a dusty, rusty yellow bus to San Pedro Sacatepéquez, a Mayan town a few miles from Guatemala City. There, and in seven other Mayan hamlets in the western highlands, I discovered the vibrant celebration of life and tradition I'd come for. In hillside villages with pastel-painted homes and whitewashed churches filled with the scent of incense, I found extended communities of living prisms. Brilliant bursts of bold colors—bright yellow, magenta, green, orange, blue, purple—saturated everything. I was dazzled.

Almost all of the textiles, from blankets and tablecloths to shirts, skirts, and headwraps, are handwoven with a profusion of those bright colors. Reminiscent of the weavings in northern Vietnam and in Indonesia, the colors and decorative motifs in some Mayan garments tell stories about the cultural background of the person wearing them. The vocabulary of colors and textiles varies from village to village. A yellow pineapple could mean health and prosperity in one, but happiness and peace in another.

Previous spread (left to right): soliciting handicrafts in Santiago Atitlan; a wedding procession in San Pedro Sacatepéquez; a handwoven *tzute* headdress.
This page: Women of Panajachal

The Maya of Guatemala are part of the larger Mayan culture that dates back to around 2000 B.C. and stretches through southern Mexico, Belize, Guatemala, and parts of Honduras and El Salvador. Sculptures, frescoes, and codices from before A.D. 1500 depict warriors and women wearing an assortment of feather, fabric, and wooden headdresses. Through the centuries, kings and noblemen were partly distinguished by their headdresses, which were shaped in cones, crowns, and spirals and often decorated with the bright green and blue feathers of the quetzal bird. One of the earliest headwraps was the *tzute*, a multipurpose cloth that could also serve as a bundle, a light blanket, or a wrap skirt. In several frescoes, tzutes were worn like headbands with the ends tied in a knot and left to hang on one side. Up until at least the early 1900s, the colors for tzutes and other textiles were harvested from nature. Brown, for instance, once came from the bark of the alder tree, purple from a sea mollusk, and red from the blood of a local insect that feeds on the tuna cactus.

In the 1500s, Spanish conquistadors arrived in the Americas, and with them, friars who sought to convert the Mayans to Christianity. In the process, they decreed that clothing should be "without adornment or color." They also ordered that all the clothes in each village conform to one style, usually distinctively different from the styles of neighboring villages. Furthermore, throughout the new Latin America women were ordered to wear veils, especially when entering a church.

The color restrictions were eventually repealed or ignored. Village-specific dress, however, prevailed. Known as *traje tipico*, these traditional Mayan costumes became external expressions of the tenacious faith of the Maya, a faith that by then had effectively combined pre-Hispanic beliefs with Catholicism. Trajes tipico are still worn by most Mayan women and by many men throughout the Guatemalan highlands. In fact, those who abandon the traje are often ridiculed as trying to blend in with Ladinos, the non-Indian population in Guatemala.

I arrived in San Pedro Sacatepéquez just as a wedding was about to start. I stood in awe outside of the church's wrought iron fence and watched as the bride, her groom, and dozens of guests filed inside. The bride wore a puffy, Western-style white gown and veil. Behind her, a crowd of well-wishers wore a glorious array of colorful traje: purple, red, and green short-sleeved tops with wide, square necks and equally colorful long wraparound skirts. Tops and skirts were made from strips of thick, handwoven textiles with abstract motifs and floral appliqués. The women had inter-

Top row: Women in the highlands interlace their braids with ribbons. The style allows them to show off their long hair, as opposed to the neatly wound turbans worn in Chichicastenango (bottom row, left and center) and in Antigua (bottom row, right).

laced pastel and neon-colored ribbons, or *listons*, into the pairs of long braids that hung down their backs, tying the ends in bows as large as grapefruits.

My next stop, Chichicastenango, was a tourists' playground a few miles further northwest. I arrived on a Saturday morning just as vendors were setting up for the town's biweekly market. Many of the vendors and shoppers came from neighboring villages and wore the traje of their individual communities. All the women wore knotted, twisted headwraps that circled their heads like halos, leaving the tops of their hair exposed. Some headwraps had thick, six-inch-long tassels and yarn puffs that bounced up and down in the back, sides, and front. Other headwraps were wound with thin ribbon and interlocking cords. Still others were made from streams of four or five separate ribbons all twisted together. Men of the Cofradias, or brother-

Top row: colorful Guatemalan yarn. Bottom row: Knotted, twisted headwraps worn in (left to right) San Antonio Palopó, Solok, Panajachel, and Chichicastenango.

hoods, wore bright red, handwoven tzutes underneath black hats with the tassels and a large corner of the fabric hanging down their backs.

I stayed in Chichi for a day, then headed south to Lake Atitlan. The lake is surrounded by three volcanoes and a dozen villages with at least three ethnic groups that have distinct languages, costumes, and cultures. In Panajachel, the first of five villages I visited around the lake, women wore blue or burgundy velvet headwraps with large knots on top. Panajachel is a sort of base camp for many tourists traveling to Lake Atitlan, so women from other villages come there to sell their handmade wares. As they walk to and from the busy square near the main dock, young women with big smiles balance bundles and stacks of dozens of blankets and scarves on their heads. "Our scarves go with everything," said one woman from Santa Catarina Palopó, who wore a royal blue headwrap with threads of shiny pink, silver, and blue string. In Santa Catarina Palopó, another woman allowed me to sit on her front porch and watch as she wound her turban. First, she gathered her hair loosely at the nape of her neck, then she wrapped the textile around it to the ends in a continuous spiral. She rolled the whole thing around her head and knotted the ends into a ball at the top.

In Santiago Atitlan, the women wear saucer-like wraps called *cintas*. They wind several yards of narrow, bright red fabric around and around their heads until they have wraps with diameters of nearly a foot wide. They are similar to turbans shown on relief figures from the Itzae ruins of Copan in southern Yucatan, Mexico.

In other parts of Lake Atitlan, I saw the same wide taffeta ribbons I'd seen in San Pedro Sacatepéquez. "This style is new but is very popular," explained a woman sitting beside me on the boat. "You will see it in many towns. Women don't always have time to weave their headwraps, and some don't like how the turbans hide their hair." Ribbons are bought ready-to-wear and come in a variety of colors that are not village specific. They quickly became popular in several highland communities and are now a recognizable part of a woman's traje, although some women who've adopted the ribbons replace them for more traditional headwraps on special occasions.

I could have stayed in Guatemala for another month without getting bored—with the country's headwraps or its people. But the United States was calling me. Before I left the highlands, I bought a blanket and several scarves. If I couldn't live in their prism, I could at least bring a piece of it home with me.

Cintas worn in Santiago Atitlan.

The United States

I didn't get a chance to call my parents much while I was traveling, but I often thought about them and the things we had done together when I was growing up. When I was a child, every summer my parents would load me and Tracy into the back of our station wagon and drive us from St. Louis to the small towns in rural Mississippi where they had been born. On the night of our arrival, my sister and I would unroll our sleeping bags on some relative's floor and listen to stories about the 1930s, '40s, and '50s. One aunt talked about chasing chickens. An uncle described the first time he'd flushed a porcelain toilet. Everyone talked about my father, who was the best marksman in the whole county, whether he was armed with a shotgun or a homemade slingshot. My mother was known for "walking the barrel," a game children with no bicycles often played using their fathers' moonshine barrels. My mom would turn a barrel on its side, give it a roll, and hop on—balancing a steady sprint sometimes for a mile or more to the store and back.

What they didn't talk much about was the work. Both of my parents and many of my relatives had picked cotton when they were young, earning about fifty cents for every pound they harvested. Six days a week—from Monday through Saturday—they worked from "can to can't," meaning their day started the minute it could, usually before sunrise, and continued after sunset when nothing more could be done. "When we got to the field, we'd each stand at the end of a row. The rows were so long, they looked like they stretched from one side of the wood to the next," my mom recalled, referring

to the distant trees that surrounded each field.

Under the stifling sun and surrounded by a countryside of clay dirt and cotton spores, most men shielded themselves with floppy, wide-brimmed hats, and women protected their hair with squares of old fabric or pieces of torn stockings. "Everyone had their hair tied up," remembered my mom. "If we didn't use a scarf or stocking on our heads, we'd be covered in dirt." Like my relatives, most southern black women who labored in the fields or as maids wore headwraps. They had little time to fuss over their appearance, so simple head ties with a single knot in the front or back came in handy. On Sundays for church, at special occasions such as weddings, baptisms, and dances, and when they went to the market, women took the time to style their hair or created more decorative headwraps by using better fabric and tying it with more flare.

Known in different regions as bandannas, head ties, headkerchiefs, head handkerchiefs, tignons, or turbans, the head coverings worn by black Americans are an offshoot of the turbans worn by West African women brought over as slaves, beginning with the first indentured servants in Virginia in 1619. Over the next two centuries, squares of light and dark cotton, as well as checked, plaid, and paisley fabrics and floral prints, were given to slave women at Christmastime in many parts of the South. The women used the gifts for head ties, among other things, shaping a wide range of styles that depended on the length of the fabric, the occasion, and their individual creativity. Many styles were quite beautiful, and when a group of women got together, they would really shine. In 1838, the English actress Frances Anne Kemble wrote from her husband's Georgian plantation that the slave women's "head handkerchiefs" put "one's very eyes out from a mile off" (John A. Scott, ed., *Journal of a Residence on a Georgian Plantation in 1838–1839*, 1984). In 1875, in his book *The Great South*, the writer Edward King wrote that South Carolina slaves "were dressed in gay colors, with handkerchiefs uniting all the colors of the rainbow, around their temples."

During this time, free black women from the West Indies brought their elaborate madras headwraps to America. Many settled in New Orleans, where the equally colorful and attractive tignon was already an important part of Creole life.

Page 194: Bandanas are seen on the streets of every American city. Page 195 (left to right): an increasingly popular, easy-to-wrap style; a Dakotah chief in a late 18th-century drawing. This page: Portrait of Marie Laveau, the "Voodoo Queen" of New Orleans wearing her *tignon*.

Worn mostly by Creoles until the late 1800s, some tignons had points similar to those of the madrases in Martinique. Others resembled fanciful mouchoirs from Guadeloupe or a variety of head ties from Haiti, but most were done in styles that were unique to New Orleans.

The fact that the tignons were so attractive was a clever response to laws and ordinances attempting to define an increasingly blurred color line. They wanted to distinguish Creole women of mixed blood from white women. Some mulattoes "were fairer than fair, with blond hair and blue eyes," explained Barbara Trevigne, a historian of New Orleans culture. In 1786, during Louisiana's Spanish period, Governor Esteban Rodriguez Miro decreed that women with any trace of African blood could no longer wear attractive coiffures; they would have to wear headwraps. There's some disagreement as to how closely women followed the law and for how long, but the tignon became an accessory among Creole women as well as among other free black women and some domestic slaves. Other slave women wore simple kerchiefs.

In 1865, when the last slaves were freed, some black women still wore head ties of some kind. Headwraps were considered crowns, especially in the church, where most women always kept their heads covered. By the early 1900s, however, as black people faced harsh racism and were flooded with negative images about Africa, head ties had become a painful reminder of the deep-rooted institution of slavery, of their African past, and of what many considered a backward culture. To get away from that culture, or rather, to invent a new American culture for themselves, many women abandoned their head ties. In the north, "do-rags" emerged in the 1920s as a tool for creating the "conk," a slick, straightened hairstyle made legendary by the jazz artist Cab Calloway. Do-rags, rarely seen in public, were generally tied with the knot in front so the back of the fabric and the ends of the hair lay flat. The fabric kept humidity from causing the hair to return to its natural curly state.

In the meantime, Native Americans were dealing with their own form of cross-

Top: Freed slaves in Savannah, 1875
Bottom: An ex-slave from New Orleans, 1885.

Traditional Native American dress at a powwow in New Mexico: a Sioux in a feather headdress (this page) and two Lakota girls in ribbon-wrapped braids (opposite page).

culturalization. Before Christopher Columbus arrived in 1492, many of America's indigenous peoples had worn feather, bead, leather, and fur headdresses for ceremonial purposes or to protect their hair and keep it out of the way. But as Europeans penetrated the countryside, they introduced a variety of fabrics, as well as varied bonnets, scarves, and hats. Over the next 200 to 300 years, as indigenous peoples made contact with Europeans, many adopted headwraps as part of their ceremonial and/or everyday dress.

One such group was the Lakota from the northern plains. Traditionally, Lakota women wrapped strips of animal hide and fur around their hair, which was usually divided into two braids. "We needed to use something to keep our hair neat and clean, and to keep our braids from unwinding. If we were in the woods collecting berries or something, our hair could get snagged if it wasn't covered," explained a Lakota woman living in Wichita, Kansas, whom I interviewed. "We preferred otter fur," she said, "especially from river trap otters, because they have a dense, compact fur that doesn't shed easily." In the 1700s, Lakota women began experimenting with fabric ties instead of fur. Today, many Lakota women and women from other indigenous nations cover their braids with long, narrow ribbons. At a powwow—a festive gathering of indigenous nations—in New Mexico, where women from at least a dozen nations wore traditional dress that included ribbon wraps, I asked a Sioux woman about the trend. She said, "When fabric was introduced, it made everything easy and convenient. I don't think anyone considered it as abandoning our culture. I think it was just seen as something new that we could use."

The ribbon wraps—which crisscross two strands of fabric back and forth from the start of the braid to the ends—have become something of an art form in themselves. The crisscross patterns create small, diamond-shaped windows that expose the women's hair. At the bottom, the ribbons come together in opposite directions, are tied in a bow or knot, and often are decorated with hand-crafted beaded barrettes. "It is difficult to wrap the ribbons around our hair by ourselves," explained the Lakota woman. "Girls often get together with their friends, and wives sometimes let their husbands do it for them. This is what my grandmother did, and her grandmother before that. When your husband does it for you, it's a sign of his love," she explained.

The new fabrics also affected men, who occasionally used cloth to make headbands and turbans. "We didn't have much fabric or wear headbands before the Europeans," noted one official at the Apache Cultural Center in Arizona. "Other Indian nations might have used buckskin to keep their hair back, but most just braided their hair and used bear oil to hold the braids in place," he said. Many Apache men, including the mid-nineteenth-century warriors Cochise and Geronimo, have been illustrated or photographed wearing headbands or headwraps.

In the 1700s, some Cherokee men began wearing turbans. In 1730, the British adventurer Alexander Cuming traveled to England with a delegation of seven Cherokee men. After first meeting the Cherokee in their native dress, which included "an apron about their middles," according to one account, and bald, tattooed heads, King George II is said to have given them more appropriate clothing for their London stay. "Their clothes were taken and replaced with jackets and European trousers," said Lisa Stopp, a teacher of Cherokee history. The Cherokee were also told to wear turbans, which were common in London at the time because of the influx of male immigrants from India. They returned to America in their new clothes and headgear. "They learned to tie the turbans themselves. Not exactly the same, so it became their own style. Their return coincided with more European contact, and white people preferred to see them like that," said Stopp. A portrait of the seven delegates in their new attire was commissioned by the Duke of Montagu, and in the years after that, portraits of Tah-chee, Sequoyah, and other Cherokee show the continued popularity of their turbans. "Turbans stayed around for years," explained a Cherokee at the Cherokee Heritage Center in Oklahoma. "It never caught on with the larger Cherokee nation, and most chiefs never wore them," he said.

In 1917, as the United States entered World War I, American women helped to replace the male workforce that had gone overseas to fight. They worked in factories,

Portrait of Dolley Madison

on railroads, in shipyards, and in other settings that required functional clothing. Many of them began wearing turbans to work. Their headwraps helped keep dust and smoke out of their hair. Not since the early 1800s, when Dolley Madison, wife of President James Madison, had brought back a turban from Paris, had headwraps been so popular among white Americans. Dolley's attraction to jeweled and feathered turbans and matching frocks cost the president $1,000 a year. She was "so addicted to those turbans," wrote the biographer Carl Sferrazza Anthony in his book *First Ladies: The Saga of the Presidents' Wives and Their Power* (1990), that "she even napped in them," making the turban Washington, D.C.'s "latest fashion rage." Aside from the occasional turbans, most white, affluent Americans wore simple headscarves to "keep from catching a chill," or as head coverings in church.

In the black community, headwraps continued to be a source of cultural identity. In the 1960s, the conk died out, and by the 1970s the do-rag was applied to the wave, a popular men's hairstyle that joined the era of Afros, braids, and headwraps that projected a new communal identity for the black community. To get their hair to ripple into rows of tiny waves, men repeatedly brushed it against the grain, then pressed it down with a nylon scarf or a pair of nylon stockings. "We'd brush our hair every day, like a hundred times," Tim Norfleet, a comedian from Brownsville, Brooklyn, told me. "The thing is, only kinky hair can make waves, so it was a way for us to celebrate who we are. If your hair doesn't naturally curl into a perfect nine it can't make waves." The brushing served to straighten out the hair for a short while, and before the hair could curl back into "the nine," or tight loops of hair, men pressed their scarves down on it so that it would flow into a wave instead.

Turbans were also embraced in the 1960s and 1970s by black nationalist organizations, authors, artists, and students. Fashionably ethnic headwraps and headscarves were worn on the streets and in rallies and were featured in nationwide advertisements and on magazine covers.

By the late 1980s, bandannas—inexpensive squares of material in bold, simple colors such as black, red, navy, and green—emerged as a popular accessory. Originally worn by prison inmates and members of street gangs in Los Angeles and New York, bandannas "made people look stronger, and more mean," explained Ruth P. Rubinstein, a professor at the Fashion Institute of Technology. The look was particularly popular among America's motorcycle gangs and inner-city youth, who both adopted specific colors to identify alliances. Gang members were (and still are) often buried with their bandannas. Families usually resist having their children buried wearing a head tie, so the bandannas are often placed in the casket alongside the body. They are also thrown on top of caskets as tokens of remembrance.

Bandannas quickly evolved into a hip-hop must-have, and by the early 1990s, they were a multicultural phenomenon. Whether worn as head ties or headbands, bandannas became everyday dress for young urban men and women of every race. Never quite able to overcome the stigma of their gang and prison origins, however, they were often banned in nightclubs and in public schools.

In the late 1990s, creative designers, such as Simone of Ms. Got Rocks in New York City, the wife of the rapper LL Cool J, made inroads by reinventing the bandanna as urban haute-couture. Her special-order creations are embellished with Austrian crystals and semi-precious gems. "I started embellishing bandannas with the crystals for myself. Then people saw me wearing them and asked if I could make some for them. Twelve women in my church wear them. I've filled orders for dozens of women in Milwaukee, Houston, and Los Angeles. I have orders for more and I've even been asked to do versions for women in Saudi Arabia," she told me. Other grassroots designers have done the same with sequins, beads, and various other miniature ornaments.

Much of America's relationship with headwraps and headscarves can be witnessed through the nation's entertainment industry. From films that try to re-create ethnic dress to entertainers who include turbans in their wardrobes, headwraps and

The bandanna was originally worn by prison inmates and gang members. Its gangster image was adopted and popularized by hard-hitting celebrities such as actor and rapper Ice Cube (above). Wrapped another way, bandannas make for hip, low-key headwraps, worn by many urban youths (below).

This chef prefers a fanciful headwrap to a traditional toque.

headscarves are seen as much on the stage and the big screen as they are on the streets. In the movies and TV shows of the 1940s and 1950s, Ann Sheridan, Rita Hayworth, and Lucille Ball wore tight turbans tied in the front with coquettish knots or bows. In the 1960s, Jimi Hendrix often wrapped a headband around the crown of his Afro. More recently, opera singers such as Leontyne Price and Jessye Norman have worn stunningly elaborate headwraps to match their diva images. The singer Erykah Badu wore tightly wound turbans towering to a height twice the size of her head for CD covers in the late 1990s, and generations of other entertainers both male and female, from Barbra Streisand, Cher, Cicely Tyson, and Ruby Dee to Bruce Springsteen, Ice Cube, India.Arie, and Eve, have been known for their attractive—and sometimes sexy and provocative—headwraps and bandanas made from rich linen, silk, cotton, and gauze fabrics.

Although celebrities can pull off wearing headwraps and headscarves pretty easily, everyday Americans often have more trouble with them. Headwraps, sometimes considered against the grain or even militant, are not always welcome in the workplace. In 1992, a Muslim flight attendant was told to remove her scarf before reporting to work, and in 2003, a Sikh lawyer visiting a prison in New Jersey was denied access to his client because he refused to remove his pagri. In an incident in Florida in 2003, a Muslim woman refused to remove the veil that covered half her face for her driver's license photo, and Sikh men have long resisted removing their turbans to wear helmets when riding motorcycles.

Most of the people I talked to in New York City who wear fashionable turbans said they would feel uncomfortable showing up at job interviews or going to work in Corporate America in their headwraps. The exceptions were people whose workplace wardrobe isn't dictated by established standards. Since 1996, a junior chef in New York named China Scantling has worn intricately wrapped turbans, instead of the traditional chef's toque of her contemporaries, to work in one of New York's hippest restaurants. "As long as I do my job," she said, "nobody bothers me." Artist and sculptor Chakaia Booker reports to no one in her Harlem studio, where she freely wears her incredibly stacked, multilayered headdresses. "People on the street always stare at me, but I see that as a connection. Whether positive or negative, it encourages some kind of communication," she said.

Artist Chakaia Booker has a headwrap look all her own.

I admire women and men who wear headwraps. I've discovered that it takes a lot of effort to find the right fabrics and colors and then to create a wrapping style. A good headwrap can emphasize all of the best features in a person's face while also making a statement about the wearer's sense of style and level of self-confidence. After a year of examining thousands of big and small turbans, somber and sassy headscarves, and the many cultures that have embraced them, I've gained a greater appreciation for my own efforts in front of the mirror. In my wrapping attempts, I join a brotherhood of world cultures and peoples that start their days with a band of fabric and a desire or need to wrap, tuck, cover, and tie. From time to time, I think back over the styles I saw during my global journey, and sometimes I try to apply some of the things I learned to my own head coverings. My versions may not be as impressive

or as authentic as the ones I remember. But if there's one thing I learned from my travels, it's that headwraps are meant to be unique. My style may not look like anyone else's, it's mine. And that's all that really matters.

Me in my headwrap.

Conclusion

I returned to New York City in July 2001. Two months later, while I was still digesting my experiences and trying to somehow figure out what they all meant, two commercial jet-liners flew into the World Trade Center and the towers collapsed, killing thousands. Muslim terrorists were blamed for the attack. Many people assumed that Muslim terrorists wear turbans, so innocent men who also wore headwraps were instantly targeted for revenge. The situation was so severe that within hours of the disaster, a Sikh friend called me at work and asked if I would get a cab and pick him up at his job. He was concerned about wearing his pagri outside alone. He could, of course, have removed his turban and simply walked outside bareheaded. But my trip to India had taught me enough about the Sikh culture to know that he would never do that. Many Sikh men refuse to even adjust their turbans to listen to headphones, let alone completely remove them, an act which for some would be akin to denying their heritage. I simply said yes and hopped into a cab to get him.

A lot of people ask me what I learned from my travels and whether I developed a favorite headwrap style. I certainly learned a lot, such as how to say hello in more than thirty languages, how to identify eleven kinds of rice, and how to recognize at least eight kinds of handwoven carpets. I remember each country by its sunsets, its strange sounds, its foods, and (of course) its unique headwraps. I discovered remarkable fabrics, sensuous textiles, elaborate motifs, and intricate embroidery. I did not really return with a favorite headwrap style, or a favorite country, although aspects of the headwraps in Senegal, Indonesia, Vietnam, and France have since crept into my recent attempts. More important, I learned that the world, despite the sins and uniformity of globalization, is still a wide and wondrous place of brilliant variety. Headwraps are just one manifestation of humankind's unending desire to decorate and define itself. I hope that you've enjoyed the journey.

Acknowledgments

While I may have traveled by myself, I gladly admit that I was never truly alone. I was constantly looked after, cared for, and watched over by God, and by a lot of people here on Earth, including longtime friends and complete strangers who made sure I was safe, warm, and on track with my goals.

I am deeply indebted to Michelle Jackson, Tracy Thompson, Robin Stone, and Leslie Powell, who were my lifeline in the States and who each played a significant role in keeping my schedule, finances, and sanity in check. I am also grateful to everyone I met abroad who embraced my project, then generously showed me their world, answered my questions, and introduced me to others. Some of them even let me stay in their homes, and for that, I say thanks to Héléne Saget, Ian Fisher, Patrick E. Tyler, Scot Sterling, Norimitsu Onishi, Mr. and Mrs. Chief Sir Johnson Okoye Igwe (Ide Awka-Etiti), Mr. and Mrs. Joginder Singh, Mr. and Mrs. John Liu, Eryka J. Berner, and Mr. and Mrs. Mustapha Ibrahim. Still others generously donated photographs or allowed themselves to be photographed. I am particularly grateful to Culver Pictures who provided more than half of the book's historical artwork, as well as to Rebecca Cooney, Stevan Harrell, Pamela Cross, Uwe Ommer, Ramesh Shukla, Huong Lieu Loan, the National Czech and Slovak Museum in Cedar Rapids, Iowa, and the Louisiana State Museum.

While abroad, I wrote a series of articles for *Essence* magazine's online edition. For that, I am grateful to Susan E. Taylor and Robin Stone.

The fact that I accomplished so much in such a short time is thanks to the advice and support I received from friends, such as Carolyn Lelyveld, and colleagues at *The New York Times*, such as Tom Bodkin, John Darnton, and several *Times* foreign correspondents. Suzanne Daley and Donald McNeil put up with me as I migrated back and forth to the Paris bureau for six months. Stephen Kinzer offered help in Istanbul and Celia Dugger was very kind in New Delhi. Patrick, Nori, and Ian from the above list not only opened their homes, but also shared their contacts in Moscow, Abidjan, and Nairobi, respectively. My gratitude extends to the amazingly efficient support staff at each of those bureaus.

Once my travels ended, dozens of people provided additional insight and valuable assistance. In addition to those already mentioned in the text, my gratitude goes to Abdoulaye Ben Ousman, Chan Vo, Mary Hardiman, Cheryl Chu, Arvind Pal Singh Mandair, Manjit Singh, Rabinder Singh, Vanessa des Vignes, Timothy Norfleet, Stephanie Rivers, Eliott Mills, Carolyn Ellison, the faculty and staff of Yeshiva University, and other generous souls all over the world who responded quickly to my many emergencies.

Lastly, I am indebted to Gerald Boyd for, among many things, a comment he made that empowered me to find my own voice, and to Kate Darnton, my editor, who helped me refine it.

To everyone else who helped but may not have been mentioned here, I couldn't have done this without you. Thank you.

Source Notes and Photography Credits

SOURCE NOTES

The information in *Headwraps* was compiled primarily from personal observations and from interviews with people native to the regions featured in the book. I received guidance from cultural and academic experts in each region. Unless information was a specific memory from an interviewee's first-hand experience, all facts were confirmed by at least two other interviews or by a published book or periodical. Below is a selection of some of the many English-language publications I consulted.

Ali, Abdullah Yusuf. *The Meaning of the Holy Qur'an.* Beltsville, MD: Amana Publications, 2002.

Altman, Patricia and Caroline West. *Threads of Identity: Maya Costume in the 1960s in Highland Guatemala.* Los Angeles: UCLA Fowler Museum of Cultural History, 1992.

Audric, John. *Siam: The Land and the People.* New York: A. S. Barnes and Company, 1969.

Canby, Sheila R. *The Golden Age of Persian Art: 1501–1722.* New York: Harry N. Abrams, Inc., 2000; British Museum Press, 1999.

Cheneviere, Alain. *Central Asia: The Sons of Tamburlaine.* Trans. AJ F. Miller. Paris: Vilo International Publishing, 2001.

Chico, Beverly. "Gender, Headwear and Power in Judaic and Christian Traditions." *Dress,* The Costume Society of America, vol. 17, 1990.

Duggal, K.S. *The Sikh People—Yesterday and Today.* New Delhi: UBS Publishers' Distributors Ltd, 1994.

Gillow, John. *Traditional Indonesian Textiles.* London: Thames and Hudson, 1992.

Hall, Gwendolyn Midlo. *Africans in Colonial Louisiana: The Development of Afro-Creole Culture in the Eighteenth Century.* Baton Rouge: Louisiana State University Press, 1995.

Hamilton, Roy W., ed. *From the Rainbow's Varied Hue: Textiles of the Southern Philippines.* Los Angeles: UCLA Fowler Museum of Cultural History, 1998.

Harrell, Stevan, Bamo Qubumo, and Ma Erzi. *Mountain Patterns: The Survival of Nuosu Culture in China.* Seattle: University of Washington Press, 2000.

Herrin, Judith. *The Formation of Christendom.* Princeton: Princeton University Press, 1987.

Historical Costumes of Turkish Women. Istanbul: Middle East Video Corp, 1986.

Hopkirk, Kathleen. *Central Asia, A Traveler's Companion.* London: John Murray Publishers, 1993.

Johnson, Rev. Samuel. *The History of the Yoruba.* Lagos: C. S. S. Bookshops Ltd. 1997.

Kinross, Lord. *The Ottoman Centuries: The Rise and Fall of the Turkish Empire.* New York: Morrow Quill, 1977.

Lissner, Ivar. *The Living Past.* Trans. J. Maxwell Brownjohn. New York: G.P. Putnam's Sons, 1957.

Lewis, Bernard, ed. *Middle East Mosaic: Fragments of Life, Letters and History.* New York: Random House, 2000.

———. *The World of Islam: Faith, People, Culture (The Great Civilizations).* London: Thames and Hudson, 1992.

Lewis, Paul and Elaine Lewis. *Peoples of the Golden Triangle: Six Tribes in Thailand.* London: Thames and Hudson, 1998.

Lindisfarne-Tapper, Nancy and Bruce Ingham. *Languages of Dress in the Middle East.* London: Curzon Press, 1997.

Longhena, Maria. *Ancient Mexico: The History and Culture of the Maya, Aztecs and Other Pre-Columbian Peoples.* New York: Stewart, Tabori and Chang, 1998.

Martineau, Harriet. *Society in America.* London: Saunders and Otley, 1837.

Magubane, Peter and Alan Mountain. *Vanishing Cultures of South Africa.* Cape Town: Struik Publishers, 1998.

McLeod, W. H. *The Sikhs History, Religion and Society.* New York: Columbia University Press, 1989.

Morris, Richard B. and Graham W. Irwin, eds. *Harper Encyclopedia of the Modern World.* New York: Harper and Row Publishers, 1970.

The New Encyclopedia of Judaism. Jerusalem: G.G. The Jerusalem Publishing House, Ltd, 1989.

Özdalga, Elisabeth. *The Veiling Issue, Official Secularism and Popular Islam in Modern Turkey.* London: Curzon Press, 1998.

Pettersen, Carmen L. *The Maya of Guatemala: Their Life and Dress.* Guatemala City: Ixchel Museum 1976.

The Qur'an. New York: Everyman's Library, 1994.

Rubens, Alfred. *History of Jewish Costumes.* New York: Funk and Wagner, 1967.

Scott, William Henry. *Barangay: Sixteenth Century Philippine Culture and Society.* Manila: Ateneo De Manila University Press, 1994.

Sharew, Worku. "Genna: Ethiopian Christmas." *Ethiopia Tourist Newsletter*, vol. 4, no. 2 (Jan-Mar 2001).

Such Is Vietnam. Hanoi: National Political Publishing House, 1995.

Summerfield, Anne and John Summerfield, eds. *Walk in Splendor: Ceremonial Dress and the Minangkabau.* Los Angeles: UCLA Fowler Museum of Cultural History, 1999.

Tandberg, Gerilyn. "Field Hand Clothing in Louisiana and Mississippi During the Antebellum Period." *Dress*, The Costume Society of America, vol. 6 (1980).

Vietnam News Agency. *Vietnam: Image of the Community of 54 Ethnic Groups.* Hanoi: Ethnic Cultures Publishing House, 1996.

Warren, William. *Thailand: The Golden Kingdom.* Hong Kong: Periplus Editions, 1999.

Wilcox, R. Turner. *Folk and Festival Costume of the World.* New York: Scribner, 1965.

———. *The Mode in Costume.* New York: Scribner, 1942

Wilds, John, Charles F. Dufour, and Walter G. Cowan. *Louisiana Yesterday and Today: A Historical Guide to the State.* Baton Rouge: Louisiana State University Press, 1996.

Williams, Marty Newman and Anne Echols. *Between Pit and Pedestal: Women in the Middle Ages.* Princeton: Markus Wiener Publishers, 1994.

PHOTOGRAPHY CREDITS

Any images not listed here were provided by the author.

Page 4   top, Culver Pictures
Page 6   Culver Pictures
Page 9   top, Culver Pictures
Page 16   Corbis
Page 17   Corbis
Page 23   bottom, Le Musée de la Femme
Page 28   Lori Waselchuk
Page 29   both photos, New Holland Publishing
Page 31   left, Darrel Plowes; right, New Holland Publishing
Page 32   top, New Holland Publishing
Page 34   right, Gerald Cubitt; left, Ian Vorster
Page 48   Ethnological Museum, Addis Ababa.
Page 52   Culver Pictures
Page 53   top two photos, Culver Pictures
Page 54   Culver Pictures
Page 55   Culver Pictures
Page 57   Culver Pictures
Page 59   Culver Pictures
Page 60   Corina Lecca
Page 61   both, Culver Pictures
Page 62   top, Culver Pictures; bottom illustration, Anita Erling
Page 63   Culver Pictures
Page 64   illustrations by Anita Erling
Page 65   Archives Hermes
Page 66   Lanvin
Page 68   Russian Library
Page 69   both, Culver Pictures
Page 70   all, Russian Library
Page 71   Culver Pictures
Page 72   Culver Pictures
Page 74   Culver Pictures
Page 75   Culver Pictures
Page 76   National Czech and Slovak Museum and Library, Cedar Rapids, Iowa
Page 77   left, George and Beth Drost, Chicago; right, National Czech and Slovak Museum and Library, Cedar Rapids, Iowa
Page 78   National Czech and Slovak Museum and Library, Cedar Rapids, Iowa
Page 79   National Czech and Slovak Museum and Library, Cedar Rapids, Iowa
Page 80   National Czech and Slovak Museum and Library, Cedar Rapids, Iowa
Page 81   bottom left, National Czech and Slovak Museum and Library, Cedar Rapids, Iowa

PublicAffairs is a nonfiction publishing house founded in 1997. It is a tribute to the standards, values, and flair of three persons who have served as mentors to countless reporters, writers, editors, and book people of all kinds, including me.

I. F. Stone, proprietor of *I. F. Stone's Weekly,* combined a commitment to the First Amendment with entrepreneurial zeal and reporting skill and became one of the great independent journalists in American history. At the age of eighty, Izzy published *The Trial of Socrates,* which was a national bestseller. He wrote the book after he taught himself ancient Greek.

Benjamin C. Bradlee was for nearly thirty years the charismatic editorial leader of *The Washington Post.* It was Ben who gave the *Post* the range and courage to pursue such historic issues as Watergate. He supported his reporters with a tenacity that made them fearless, and it is no accident that so many became authors of influential, best-selling books.

Robert L. Bernstein, the chief executive of Random House for more than a quarter century, guided one of the nation's premier publishing houses. Bob was personally responsible for many books of political dissent and argument that challenged tyranny around the globe. He is also the founder and was the longtime chair of Human Rights Watch, one of the most respected human rights organizations in the world.

·   ·   ·

For fifty years, the banner of Public Affairs Press was carried by its owner Morris B. Schnapper, who published Gandhi, Nasser, Toynbee, Truman, and about 1,500 other authors. In 1983 Schnapper was described by *The Washington Post* as "a redoubtable gadfly." His legacy will endure in the books to come.

Peter Osnos, *Publisher*